"Are you struggling to engage with your kids in an era of smartphones, hectic schedules, and cultural confusion? David Eaton and Jeremiah Callihan are here to help. With great wisdom and a genuine heart for today's teens, they offer keen, biblically based insight that parents will find invaluable."

—Jim Daly, president of Focus on the Family

"David and Jeremiah understand the next generation. And they are passionate about helping you parent well. So listen to what they have to say! And allow them to serve as your coaches on connecting with teenagers today. Better parenting starts now!"

—Brad Lomenick, founder of BLINC and author of *The Catalyst Leader* and *H3 Leadership*

"I love this book. *Engaging Your Teen's World* is a positive, practical, and powerful book. Since it is written by parents and youth culture experts, this book will help you better understand student culture today and equip you to effectively engage the teenagers in your life. I highly recommend it."

—Sean McDowell, PhD, associate professor at Biola University, speaker, and coauthor of *So the Next Generation Will Know*

"Say good-bye to guilt, frustration, and sullen silence. *Engaging Your Teen's World* is a game changer in understanding your kids and engaging them through curiosity and common sense. David Eaton and Jeremiah Callihan from Axis are trusted 'culture translators' who demystify teen culture with proven, practical advice."

—Jeff Myers, PhD, president of Summit Ministries

"In this culture, every parent of teens needs an offensive game plan to guide and protect their teens through one of the most dangerous seasons of their lives. Eaton and Callihan's book will empower you with the vison, courage, and wisdom you need to disciple your sons and daughters to become mature and productive followers of Christ."

—Dr. Dennis Rainey, founder of FamilyLife

"This book is full of clarity and practical—really practical—advice. Parents, youth workers, grandparents, and anyone with a teenager in their life would do well to absorb the wisdom here."

—John Stonestreet, president of the Colson Center and coauthor of *A Practical Guide to Culture*

ENGAGING YOUR TEEN'S WORLD

Understanding What Today's Youth
Are Thinking, Doing, and Watching

DAVID EATON AND
JEREMIAH CALLIHAN
WITH ALAN BRIGGS

BETHANYHOUSE
a division of Baker Publishing Group
Minneapolis, Minnesota

© 2020 by Axis

Published by Bethany House Publishers
11400 Hampshire Avenue South
Bloomington, Minnesota 55438
www.bethanyhouse.com

Bethany House Publishers is a division of
Baker Publishing Group, Grand Rapids, Michigan

Printed in the United States of America

Library of Congress Cataloging-in-Publication Data
Names: Eaton, David, President of Axis, author. | Callihan, Jeremiah, CEO and
    cofounder of Axis, author. | Briggs, Alan, author.
Title: Engaging your teen's world : understanding what today's youth are thinking,
    doing, and watching / David Eaton.
Description: Minneapolis, Minnesota : Bethany House Publishers, 2020.
Identifiers: LCCN 2019056302 | ISBN 9780764235825 (trade paperback) |
    ISBN 9781493425273 (ebook)
Subjects: LCSH: Parent and teenager—Religious aspects—Christianity.
    | Teenagers—Religious life. | Teenagers—Psychology.
Classification: LCC BV4529 .E26 2020 | DDC 248.8/45—dc23
LC record available at https://lccn.loc.gov/2019056302

Cover design by Brand Navigation

20 21 22 23 24 25 26   7 6 5 4 3 2 1

To my parents.

—David

To the reason God put me here to care about having
one lifelong conversation: Nehemiah, Elijah, Jonathan,
and Mari. To the one helping me have that one lifelong
conversation: my amazing wife, Kim.

—Jeremiah

To the parents and grandparents
courageously raising the rising generation.

Contents

Section 4: What Now?

Introduction

We Know You Care

If you're cracking open these pages, you care about a teenager. You are a parent, grandparent, teacher, coach, student pastor, mentor, or youth worker. Perhaps your greatest tool in shaping the soft clay of their lives is the simplest tool you wield: *You care*. You care enough to worry about them, have hard conversations with them, invest your precious time into them, discipline them, pray for them, and pick up a book like this one to learn how you can help them. And if you don't actually do all those things, you want to.

Chances are that someone cared for you as you navigated your turbulent and insecure teenage years. Perhaps a teacher spoke vision into you, a coach challenged you to dig deep, a parent reached past your destructive behavior, or a grandparent made you feel like you were worth loving. A moment of care or belief can change everything! We all need someone to care about us and believe in us when we are young. Care is vital, but unfortunately, it's not enough. You're going to need more tools in your tool belt.

Teens have a bad reputation. Too often we talk down about them. We have low expectations of them, and many times they live up to that low bar we've set. You had better believe they pick up on our lack of confidence in them. Many of us have believed lies that teens are full of problems, and that we just need to wait it out so they can limp into adulthood. Youth expert Sharon Galgay Ketcham says, "We problematize teenagers and use significant resources to try to fix them. This narrative evokes fear and, in loving response, parents are desperate to keep them safe. . . . Teenagers are more than problems to be solved—they have potential as human beings."[1] Our Axis team of culture translators and parent research assistants agrees!

Teens are also battling massive issues. There are apps, troubling videos, sexual images, and cyber bullying entering their world through smartphones. There are opioids, Adderall, marijuana, and vapes entering their bloodstream. There are mental health, depression, and anxiety issues welling up inside their brains. They live in a noisy world clamoring for their attention. Your blood pressure is probably rising as you read this. You probably wonder how you can talk about God, the Gospel, the church, and the family in a culture crowded with these vices. Keep reading. We've got good news!

We want to make our motives clear; we want you to move from a caring adult in the life of a teen to a confident influencer of your teen. Our Axis team helps tens of thousands of parents understand teen culture every week, and we want to equip you to join the teens you care about on their journey into lifelong faith. Think of us as your research assistants. God put them in your life and you in their life on purpose. We believe in you, and we want to help you. We want to watch your confidence and passion for discipling your teen spike like it has for tens of thousands of parents. We want to help you engage your teen's world.

Our team creates a lot of content, too much to cram it all into this book. We organized the book into four sections: Why Engaging Your Teen's World Matters, How to Engage with Your Teen, Topics You Need to Engage with Your Teen, and What Now? We share practical knowledge and next steps, but we only scratch the surface in some areas. Don't worry, at the end of the book, we recommend resources to dig deeper into many of these topics.

We aim to encourage and equip you for the role God has given you.

Thanks for letting us into your journey with the teen you're crazy about.

—David Eaton, Axis president and cofounder, and
Jeremiah Callihan, Axis CEO and cofounder

WHY ENGAGING YOUR TEEN'S WORLD MATTERS

1

You Are a
Third-Way Parent

Young people are open and at a place where caring adults are still important in their lives—something that seems to hold true across all studies of youth and adolescents.

Daniel White Hodge, Center for Youth Ministry Studies[1]

Tell your children about it in the years to come, and let your children tell their children. Pass the story down from generation to generation.

Joel 1:3 NLT

The average adult says they only have about one spiritual conversation a year.

The Barna Group[2]

In 2007 Steve Jobs walked onto a stage in San Francisco wearing his iconic outfit; jeans, a black turtleneck, and gray New Balance shoes. The crowd waited with bated breath, anticipating his announcement. "This is a day I've been looking forward to for two and a half years. Every once in a while, a revolutionary product comes along that changes everything."

The moment he let out the secret that Apple would be releasing a "revolutionary mobile phone," the crowd cheered. His next statement was nothing short of prophetic: "Today Apple is going to reinvent the phone."[3] That same year Netflix shifted from sending DVD packets in the mail to streaming movies. Not only did phones, mobile internet access, and media consumption change in 2007, our whole culture changed.

Amidst the technology buzz, we at Axis were hatching our own plan. We were burdened for the next generation to follow Jesus into lifelong faith. Axis was birthed from our desire to see the next generation develop lifelong faith. Just like the iPhone, we had conceived the idea of Axis years before, but in 2007 we welcomed it into the world. The Axis story line has been intertwined with the smartphone ever since. We don't think it's an accident.

While technology has been changing for some time, smartphones introduced a level of change and complexity our world has never experienced before. That moment seemed to spin the earth faster on its axis (see what we did there?). Since then our team has been inviting teens, parents, and other caring adults to engage in this journey instead of simply fighting it or running from it.

While the story line of our ministry matters to us, this book isn't about us or about the past. It's about you and your future. If you're reading this, you're probably a caring adult—a parent, grandparent, pastor, coach, teacher, or mentor to a teen. This book is about you and your relationship with the teen (or teens) you care about. Amidst all the bad news and negativity, scrolling news tickers and social media feeds, we believe there is hope. There is good news in these pages for you. You've got a job to do, and we are here to help.

Two Stories, One Mission

Jeremiah and I were in our early twenties when the smartphone and Axis emerged. As a couple of zealous young guys, we saw the problem from the inside out: most teens aren't growing into a lifelong faith; they are growing out of it. Our stories are very different, but our burning passion for teens to experience a lifelong faith is the same.

I (David) came from what you might characterize as "the stable family." Every family has issues, of course, but my family is intact and more than functional. I learned lifelong faith at home. I won the parenting lottery. My parents were unassuming and gave me significant time growing up. My mom quit working as a teacher when I was born to work even harder as a full-time mom. As Lindsey and I raise our own kids, I think of that decision every week.

I'll also never forget an ironic celebration for my father at the dinner table when I was in elementary school. My dad was a police officer and received a promotion. But when you grow in seniority as an officer it means you get the bad shifts. So he turned down seniority. My mom made a shrimp dinner (this Texas kid had never seen a shrimp before) and announced, "Today is special! Your father turned down a promotion so he wouldn't have to work nights and weekends and he can be with us." I'll never forget eating shrimp dinner in the heart of Texas celebrating that promotion he turned down. My parents sacrificed much for us.

My parents were faithful, and they walked with Jesus. They raised me around the church with plenty of opportunities to serve within the congregation. In the mornings I would find my dad reading his Bible as he ate his Raisin Bran. The sex talk was blunt and without shame. I had an overzealous edge to my faith, and they helped me tone that down. Perhaps the seeds of this urgency for a generation to know Jesus were already in my bones. I was learning to work out the Gospel in the context of home, family, school, and the local church.

We ask a powerful question at Axis: *What breaks your heart and baffles your mind?* My heart breaks as I look back at my friends from high school. We went to church camp together, served on mission trips, huddled together to pray, and shared our faith. I still have a picture from a mission trip showing our team with our Bibles in hand, preaching the Gospel on a busy street corner. Since then, many of my friends have been stripped threadbare by life—many of them divorced, one of them dead, a lot of heartbreak, and three of them who were preaching in the picture with me are now atheists. Somehow the passion and zeal for Jesus didn't stick. They chucked their faith and went on with their lives.

Jeremiah had a different texture to his family.

I (Jeremiah) weathered a disorienting tapestry of experiences, moves across the country, and strange church experiences in search of the perfect spiritual environment. My parents were Christ-followers who put my siblings and me into intense environments to grow our dedication to God. The only problem was that these environments emphasized fear and legalism. Still, there was much goodness in my family and in the connected faith communities we were part of. But the pain that began in these very legalistic environments marked me.

My faith grew through a youth group, leadership on basketball teams, conversations with my parents and more conversations with my peers (including my future wife, Kimberly), studying apologetics, and environments where reason and faith collided. My faith and maturity grew amidst the tensions I experienced. My mind latched on to the words of C. S. Lewis, modern apologists, and courses that cultivated my worldview. All the while my heart for the next generation developed. Older men showed me the way, some of whom didn't even follow the life of Jesus.

My parents certainly were not perfect, but they did many things well. One thing I'm forever grateful to them for is sending me to Summit Ministries (which we are huge fans of) for a two-week worldview immersion. They also encouraged me to go to the Focus on the Family Institute, where I met David and my wife. Without those two organizations, Axis would not exist. I am so grateful my parents pushed me to do both.

My parents divorced when I was a young husband and father in my mid-twenties. Of course, it's still painful, but I will continue to fight to be a faith-filled husband and father. What I still want, to this day, is a lifelong conversation with my parents, despite their divorce and the pain this caused me as a young man. My heart beats to help parents and teens develop a lifelong faith.

Our stories are very different, but they led us to the same mission: *helping teens develop a lifelong faith.* We watched friends drift from their faith. Instead of trying to sidestep faith barriers, we have observed that we've always talked openly about them. We've even leveraged them as mechanisms for captivating an audience and starting conversations. We've chosen to take a redemptive posture on culture that doesn't condemn it or run from it. We'll share more about that third way of parenting throughout the book.

Very few people are starting meaningful conversations to translate culture through the lens of the Gospel. Even fewer were doing this a decade ago. So, our team developed creative ways to present the Gospel in language that resonates with teens. We used youth culture as a jumping-off point. It was different. It made sense. It was coming through voices of the generation they could identify with. And it was fruitful.

We still help teens cultivate lifelong faith, but our approach has changed. We are dads to amazing kids and husbands to amazing women. We spend our best energy infusing lifelong faith into our kids. Becoming dads shifted our perspective. Instead of investing most of the weeks seeking direct impact on teens, we shifted to investing our best time into equipping you, caring adults, to understand your teen's world and connect with their heart so *you* can disciple them.

Our team still engages culture and sends teams around the country to talk with kids about the intersection of faith, culture, and their decisions. We still want to inspire teens, but now we focus on helping you to help teens cultivate lifelong faith. Think of us as your research assistants.

Many of our team members have kids, even grandkids, of our own. We feel your stresses, fears, joys, and inadequacy every day. We wrestle with the rapidly changing culture and the trends we write about. We want to help! We're in your corner! We do what we're called to do so you can do what you're called to do. Our team will continue to create resources to help you cultivate conversations with the teens you love so they can walk the journey of faith for the long haul.

We know you have a desire to cultivate lifelong faith in this teen you care about. If given the chance, we know you would have meaningful conversations about the best and worst things they are experiencing. All the caring adults we interact with desire good things for the teens they love, but many are hitting barriers along the way. Here are the common barriers we observe getting in the way for caring adults.

Overwhelm

The number of things to learn about youth culture can be overwhelming. Can't it?! There is an ever-growing pile of apps, slang, shows, trends, and vices teens are engaged in that you're probably struggling to keep up with. One dad told us, "I always feel three apps behind my kid!" Can you relate? This struggle to keep your head above water can lead to a gnawing sense of being overwhelmed. Many times, as parents, we want to throw up our hands, stop trying to understand this culture enveloping our kids, and quit. It's too hard, too nuanced. We feel your pain! We have an amazing team at Axis spanning four decades who put serious energy into researching culture every week so you don't have to.

Fear

Fear has been no stranger to parents throughout history, but the fear swirling around parents today is greater than ever. It's right in our faces! It's hard to go a day without hearing a story that scares us to the core. To complicate things even more, nearly every corner of culture is changing at warp speed. Apps get outdated while new ones appear in moments. It's hard to know what we should try to keep our kids away from, let alone how to actually keep them from it.

Cultural Disconnection

All parents feel the divide between what we discuss, listen to, read, and watch and what our kids are consuming. To some degree, it's always been this way with teens (just take a moment to remember the gap you and your parents experienced). But the divide is widening with the volume of information and the rate of change today. Parents feel like they are speaking a different language and living in different subcultures, because we are.

Cluelessness

We want to be careful here, but we bet there are areas of parenting you don't have a clue about—most of them not your fault. Perhaps your parents didn't have the hard conversations with you, so you don't know how to have them with your kids. Perhaps divorce pulled your family apart and left you under-resourced. Maybe you feel like all the other parents took a master class in parenting and you never got the invite. Every parent is working from a deficit in some area. Let's be honest: Many days it would be easier to be in our cubicle at work, where we are an appreciated expert, rather than to head home, where we feel inadequate and clueless. Parenting teens is not for the weak.

We understand these pressures. We are in your corner. We want to help you connect with the teen you love. We want to help you cross the chasm to their heart, to understand the culture the teen you love is swimming in. That's why we exist. While transmitting research to parents is a huge help, we have something even deeper in mind: connecting to the heart of the teen you love. We believe a heart connection gives you the best chance to pass on lifelong faith to them. Many parents and caring adults feel the task is impossible. They've seen the numbers. The Pinetops Foundation reports that 35 million Christian teens will leave Christianity by 2050 if nothing changes, and that number could be 42 million if trends worsen.[4] But we intend for something to change. It's time for a wave of parents to push through their fears and barriers and disciple their kids. "Losing" our kids during the teen years isn't inevitable. Our team loves hearing connection stories. Recently a mom sent us a message (with a lot of smiling emojis) saying, "It's working! I'm actually connecting with my kid again!" We want that for you too.

Three Postures of Parenting

This growing fear about kids exiting the Christian faith is real. Every parent feels fear, but sometimes it spikes. Your mind wonders and wanders: *What are they looking at on their phone? Are they doing things I don't know about? What boundaries are appropriate? Am I an awful parent for not knowing what I don't know about what they're consuming?* If you're asking those questions, you're normal. The fear and sense of being overwhelmed is real. But it shouldn't drive you. We want to help your love for your teen drive you instead of your fear.

We don't pretend that the world is perfect and that there is nothing to fear. But how are you going to react to that fear? If you become engulfed in it, you won't connect with the heart of your teen. People have two basic, and very different, reactions to fear: fight or flight. Let's see how they manifest in parenting.

The fight posture

This impulse leads parents to hunker down with high-powered artillery aimed at the teen years. You will overprotect and declare war against anything that could possibly harm or negatively influence your kid. There are a few problems with this. Not only is it exhausting, but you will be on high alert during one of the best windows of time to connect with your teen. Your kid will catch at least a few stray bullets as you try to pick off any impending threats. Sometimes you (and they) will forget you're trying to protect them from something, and instead of fighting *for* your kid, you will be fighting *with* your kid. As they navigate the teenage journey, you will become more aware of the areas where you have less control than you thought. You won't give them the responsibility they need to grow in maturity.

The flight posture

The flight impulse leads you to run. You'll give up on connecting with your teen's world, and you'll miss their heart in the meantime. You'll hear whispers of the tantalizing lie, "It's an impossible game. It will take too much energy, and you can't win anyway." It's much easier to disengage from their fast and overwhelming culture and wait for them to pop out of the time machine in their twenties. This will certainly create less friction at home, and your child will have more freedom. But this road leads to the same place as the fight impulse: disengagement. It seems better than trying to control your teen out of fear, but you will disengage with your child's heart in the process.

The third way: engagement

The good news is there is a third option. A way that steers clear of white-knuckling the teenage years out of fear and trying to close your eyes until they're gone. Third-way parents choose to engage with their teen's world (and the culture they are surrounded with) so they can connect with their heart. If you want to learn to become a third-way parent, we are here to help. We want to be the first to welcome you to the messy middle. There's life here! There's connection here. We don't exist simply to help caring adults understand youth culture so you can control your teen's world. We want to help parents and caring adults engage with the teen they love so their hearts connect. Ultimately, we want to see your teen live out a lifelong faith. We bet you want that too.

Parenting is tough. There's always going to be something new. There's always going to be something you struggle with, something you've never heard of, new territory. It's hard to feel behind and out of control. Perhaps you feel helpless as a parent, misunderstood, ill-equipped, or unprepared. But if you are a parent, God has shaped the soul that has been birthed or adopted into your family.

Third-way parents have a growth mindset. They keep learning. They adapt. They are willing to look at themselves and ask, *Am I part of the problem? Are my kids on their phone all the time because they see me on my phone all the time? How do I need to grow as a parent so my kid can grow in their faith?* We love hearing from parents who are growing.

It should breathe hope into you just to hear there is this third option.

Jesus lived the third way of engagement. He could never quite claim one side, and one side could never quite claim him. He was misunderstood by the religious elite, the Jews, the non-Jews, even his disciples and his own family. He was with "the wrong people," notorious sinners, at parties—always giving the knuckleheads another chance. He lived in tension between the power of Rome, the religion of Jerusalem, and the small-town expectations of Galilee.

Jesus is our guide and example, but we also pull from the wisdom of Solomon. God has given parents and caring adults the opportunity to wrestle with the heart of the issue while connecting with the heart of this teen you love the snot out of. Jesus promised that the Holy Spirit would lend us wisdom, power, and truth for this parenting journey. And we have God's Word as a light for the rocky footpath. So, parents and caring adults, if you are seeking to lead your teen toward Jesus, you aren't alone.

2

The Most Important Conversation

Sometimes the smallest things take up the most room in our heart.

Winnie-the-Pooh

Showing interest in your kids isn't something you do; it must become who you are.

Mark Gregston[1]

The mistake most of us make in our crucial conversations is we believe that we have to choose between telling the truth and keeping a friend.

Crucial Conversations[2]

One of the saddest byproducts of the corrosion of culture is the breakdown of the family. A woman in her early thirties once shared with our team, "I've had only one real conversation with my dad."

One. Real. Conversation. Are you serious? When she said this, we were dumbfounded. If the rising generation is having only one real conversation with their parents, no wonder the Gospel is being lost in translation.

But there is a beautiful twist to this story. After saying she has had only one real conversation with her dad, she paused, and with a sweet smile said, "We've never stopped having that one conversation." Wow! She had been having a thirty-year conversation with her dad. From the looks of it, her dad is planning on having that "one conversation" with her the rest of their lives. They've talked about countless subjects, but they've been riffing on the same conversation.

Your teen may have an eighteen-month conversation with a youth pastor, a four-year conversation with a coach, or a ten-year conversation with your pastor. But with you, the parent, your child can have a sixty-year conversation. No one will ever be more influential than you. It's true when you look at sociology, history, and the Bible. This is the most important conversation of their lives. After our initial shock about this one conversation, something clicked. It made total sense to us.

You only need to have one conversation with your kid, ever. Here's the trick: It has to be ongoing. You'll pop in and out of it. You'll have it on road trips and before bed and while you're dropping them off at school and after you've picked them up at a friend's house in tears and when they want to quit on geometry and as they say they hate you because you're moving to another state.

This one conversation is a relational dance. It's a story line that runs through many scenes in one book. It's a single thread woven into a beautiful tapestry—an invitation to have many micro conversations about any subject because every one of them is part of a macro story. You start this conversation, and you continue it for a lifetime. It's the way to your kid's heart.

We want to inspire this lifelong run-on conversation and equip you to keep it going. This subtle change in perspective about having one long conversation can turn parental pressure into parental opportunity.

What's Your Flavor of Conversation?

I (David) experienced the one conversation firsthand. My mom had a conversation trick: When I was a teen she took me to Braum's, my favorite ice cream and burger joint, for a strawberry milk shake. This is the most important conversation I've ever had. Of course, I would spill my guts to her. Smart woman! She created the environment and the right kind of curiosity for me to talk. On the way to school we practiced Bible verses, trading off every other word. My dad was approachable, but not pushy. We had conversations in the back yard with baseball gloves on our hands. But it was all one conversation with many pieces and in many locations.

I (Jeremiah) had some of my most formative moments on car rides. Whether driving across town or across the country, my parents were intentional in starting conversations on theology and worldview. This wise plan to discuss deep things while I and my siblings were a captive audience will shape me forever. Now I'm seeking to redeem the copious amounts of time I am in the car with my kids—redeem the time and the miles.

There are so many flavors and ways to have this conversation. What is it for you? Baseball, the car, strawberry milk shakes, camping, tacos? Make it fit your personality and your teen's desires. Pull the thread of your kid's heart. It's going to be different for every caring adult. What's the lubricant to the conversation?

Conversation is the heartbeat of relationship. Friends who never talk drift apart. Couples who never talk grow distant. First dates with nothing to talk about don't lead to second dates. Parents and kids who don't talk about the small things don't talk about the big things. The best conversations have variety and depth.

One Message

Eugene Peterson pastored local congregations for decades and wrote more than fifty books. The Peterson home, perched on the rocks above beautiful Flathead Lake in Montana, was a refuge for weary pastors, old friends, uninspired writers, and flailing leaders. Eugene was known as the pastor to pastors but is most well known for his paraphrase of the Bible, *The Message*, which has sold millions of copies. The relevance and wonder of the poetic retelling whispers to many.

One of these was Bono, U2's front man, global advocate, and change maker. Bono was deeply impacted by Eugene. Bono invited Eugene to join him for theological conversations on tours, and the Petersons continued the conversation with Bono at their dinner table overlooking the calm waters.

Eugene was also an engaged father. Perhaps the most touching thing about Eugene's life was a story his son, Leif, told at his memorial service.

When I was in high school I used to joke with my dad that he only had one sermon. And although it was a joke between us, I believed then, as I do now, that it is largely accurate. My dad had one message. . . .

> For fifty years you've
> been telling me the secret. For fifty
> years you'd steal into my room
> at night and whisper softly to my
> sleeping head. It's the same message
> over and over and you don't vary
> it one bit.
> God loves you.
> He's on your side.
> He's coming after you.
> He's relentless.[3]

He had only one sermon. He had only one conversation with his kids. He might have fooled friends and congregants, but he didn't fool his son. It wasn't thousands of sermons, discussions, and prayers; it was one message, and he never stopped sharing it.

In the Car, the Kitchen, the Stands, and the Tent

There is a passage in the Old Testament known as the Shema. To this day, this is not simply a Scripture—it's an organizing message that pulls Jewish culture together. It's a call to bring their kids up in the faith and pass it on.

> "Hear, O Israel: The Lord our God, the Lord is one. You shall love the Lord your God with all your heart and with all your soul and with all your might. And these words that I command you today shall be on your heart. You shall teach them diligently to your children, and shall talk of them when you sit in your house, and when you walk by the way, and when you lie down, and when you rise. You shall bind them as a sign on your hand, and they shall be as frontlets between your eyes. You shall write them on the doorposts of your house and on your gates."
>
> Deuteronomy 6:4–9 ESV

This message should live in everything we do (heart, soul, might) and should be passed on to the next generation by parents. The words of God are overflowing with life. They can be branded on signs in our homes, but they are also portable. *The Message* paraphrase of this passage (emphasis added) can be particularly helpful to you as a parent:

> "Love God, your God, with your whole heart: love him with all that's in you, love him with all you've got! Write these commandments that I've given you today on your hearts. **Get them inside of you and then get them inside your children. Talk about them**

wherever you are, sitting at home or walking in the street; talk
about them from the time you get up in the morning to when you
fall into bed at night. Tie them on your hands and foreheads as a
reminder; inscribe them on the doorposts of your homes and on
your city gates."

Where does life happen for your family? Wherever that is it is
sure to be chaotic, but there is also life in those spaces. It's the
stress of herding the kids into the Suburban for church. It's a
drive back from a volleyball game where your daughter's team
got crushed in two quick sets. It's in the kitchen grabbing snacks
between Netflix episodes. It's texting with your kids while they
are at school. It's when you choose to listen to your teen's music
with them in the car instead of popping in your earbuds. It's
when you're camping and your kids won't shut up in the tent. It's
when you and your teen are both frustrated at math homework
close to midnight.

These are all little glimpses of connection. This is where life
happens, and this is where you can discuss life's most important
topics. Lean in to them to talk about life and faith and relationships and anything they want to discuss. You're going to miss these
frustrating moments when your house is empty.

Sometimes their desires as teens (and ours as parents) are misplaced. These moments can be redemptive as well. Conversations
about makeup can turn into conversations about identity. The
desire to make the traveling basketball team so they can be re-
cruited to a Division 1 school can turn into conversations about
influence. Conversations about the college success ladder can turn
into explorations of their gifts.

Our teens want to be beautiful, brave, adventurous, and independent. These conversations require the fuel of curious questions.
They need redemptive nudges. There is great news: You're with
them in those gritty, unfiltered moments, and we want to help you
fold them into one large conversation.

A Call to Action with a Promise Attached

After Jesus rose from the dead and reappeared to his disciples, he had some reminders for them. Perhaps you've already heard this call to make disciples, but we want to set this passage in context for you as parents.

> Jesus, undeterred, went right ahead and gave his charge: "God authorized and commanded me to commission you: Go out and train everyone you meet, far and near, in this way of life, marking them by baptism in the threefold name: Father, Son, and Holy Spirit. Then instruct them in the practice of all I have commanded you. I'll be with you as you do this, day after day after day, right up to the end of the age."
>
> Matthew 28: 18–20 MESSAGE

This is both a command and an invitation for you as a parent. A very simple translation of the call to making disciples from the Great Commission is this: to learn Jesus, to obey Jesus, and to reproduce Jesus into others.[4] Physical reproduction has already happened with your kid, but spiritual reproduction is always happening. It's generational, and it's God plan for us to pass it along.

We have a secret. We're just as interested in you as a parent having a vibrant faith as we are in your kids having one. When we fill ourselves with the words, wisdom, and presence of Jesus, it becomes easier to pass on faith to our kids. We want you to build your lifelong faith and become a conduit of God's grace to your kids. Are there guarantees? No. Will you model perfection for your kids? No. Do you need God to fill you up in order for that faith to overflow to your kids? You bet! Youth pastors, mentors, and Young Life leaders are not the main channel to pass on lifelong faith; that's your role. We want to help you.

Wayne Cordeiro says, "You can teach what you know, but ultimately, you are going to reproduce what you are."[5] This is equal parts encouraging and scary. We think this is good news. Ever feel like your kids just aren't hearing what you're saying? Every parent does. But when their ears are clogged (or blocked by their AirPods) they can't help but see your life. If you are living in obedience to God, your kids will see it. Trust me, even if they are awful listeners at times, they are great observers.

Parenting can feel lonely. Jesus understood that the disciples would feel lonely, so he left the Holy Spirit to be our guide. The Holy Spirit gives comfort, power, and wisdom. You're going to need all three to be a third-way parent who chooses to engage in a relationship with your child. Jesus sent the Holy Spirit, which means His presence is always with us. He is promising you, as a parent, his presence, comfort, power, and wisdom in your relationship with your teen.

Having Your One Conversation

A beautiful couple received the calling to adopt. They knew that as their two children got older, the conversations would get more complicated. They knew conversation would be crucial for their family. As their kids grew, they carved out time for conversation, but they had no idea what to talk about with them. Sound familiar?

What conversations would their kids want to be part of? With some focus and intention (and a little help from our team), they began having culturally relevant conversations. Discussion became normal, easier, and relevant. To their surprise, their kids wanted to talk. The father even got some dad points the time he taught them the latest slang for ecstasy.

Through persistence and the grace of God, the message of the love of God sank in with their kids. Their kids didn't always like their answers, but they built trust. God doesn't waste those moments of conversation. They are closer to their kids and excited for what the future holds.

These stories light us up! It's why we do what we do. We want to hear more stories of parents partnering with God to start and continue the conversations that God will build on over the years. Parents who are risking conversation with their kids are our heroes. They have adopted the posture of engaging in their teens' culture, not condemning or running away from it.

In the Trenches (or the Abyss) with Them

Mark Gregston is a grandparent who runs a home for teens in Texas. Families bring their children from across the country to spend time there for healing and wholeness. They call him "the teen whisperer." He encourages parents to create a relational atmosphere and be direct. Don't know what's getting in the way of you and your teen? "Ask them," he advises.[6] Perhaps you are doing something that is unintentionally pushing your teen away. If you really want to know, your teens will tell you. Family discussion and conversation is so important. Mark goes on to counsel, "When your children enter their teen years, you must switch your model of influence from teaching to training," and encourages parents to move from giving lectures to hosting discussions.[7]

This all sounds scary—changing the model, doing less teaching, learning more about their world. You're going to feel like you're losing control, but you're gaining trust. Here's a secret: We have way less control of our teens than we think we do. Remember, there is another choice beyond avoiding youth culture or fighting it. You can jump into the abyss of teen culture with your child without sheltering or shaming them. It's one of the scariest things you can do, but it could be the best decision you make during their teen years.

Remember that raw passion for kids to find lifelong faith that led us to launch Axis? As two young passionate leaders, we both really cared about our faith and worked hard to own it personally. We saw how good that was, but we were grieved that so many others didn't see the same thing we did. We just wanted to do right by God and wanted to know him more. God had us on that path, and we were frustrated that other kids we grew up with lost their passion and excitement for what we knew was our ultimate reality.

Now we look our own kids in the eyes, do homework with them, and pray over them before bed. Before we think about helping you pass on faith to your kids, we're trying to do that with ours. We experience the same fears you do, but we're trying to live out third-way parenting. We're trying to fend off gripping fear and debilitating apathy and engage in conversation. These conversations are the seeds of discipleship with our kids. We're having conversations in living rooms, fast food joints, and minivans.

I (Jeremiah) am coming to terms with my own difficult church experience and broken family narrative. God is using my disorienting story line of misguided fear to shape me and my family. As Axis headed into our thirteenth year of ministry, we prepared to gather our team, some champions of our cause, and a few spiritual heroes, including Ravi Zacharias, for a few days. I was tasked with sharing how my story had shaped the Axis story. Instead of a keynote I wrote a letter to my kids and read it to this group. I was reminded again how God doesn't waste our pain, our learning, our experiences. God shaped me amidst the mess and sometimes despite it.

My story is a mix of beauty and brokenness, but here I am on the other side of a lot of pain, walking with Jesus. Somehow God used revival meetings, theologians, way too many cross-country moves, legalistic environments, incredible teachers, a small Christian college, and a confusing concoction of religious experiences to shape me as a man and a father.

I've thought I was a failure at sharing Jesus at some points along the journey. Somehow God used my deep-seated desire to share the Gospel with the lost and disciple the young and old alike. Perhaps I'm not the failure I've felt I was many times. God has used the last thirty years of my life to contribute to a bigger story, to reach a place where the ministry of Axis is positioned to evangelize the lost and disciple the young and old in a way few are positioned to do.

My oldest son is a teenager. My wife and I also have three other amazing kids growing up close behind. Deuteronomy 6 continues to be the guiding text in our family and in Axis. This is the model God created to impact humanity. And we, as parents, have the ability to help write God's law on the hearts of our kids. But ultimately, I'm selfish in all of this. What I didn't know years ago when I started this is that Axis is for me. Not just because I desperately want to experience a lifelong faith and want my kids to have a lifelong faith through one lifelong conversation with me. But because God is not looking for a tidy family story or a theology degree. He is looking for parents who are obedient to make disciples in their own family.

How's Your Parental Posture?

Our body language conveys most of our message. We respond to every movement of the posture of someone across a table from us. If they lean in, we know they're curious. If they slouch and glance away, we realize they're bored. Posture matters a lot!

What's your parental posture? What body language are you sending to your teen? Are you a curious listener? Are you too distracted to go below the surface? Are you more interested in their faith growing or their landing on the honor roll? We believe it's possible for you to jump into the abyss of teen culture with your teen without sheltering or shaming them. It's possible, and it's crucial.

In the last chapter we talked about three parenting paths: fearful, passive, and engaged. We want to help you become a third-way parent with the posture of engagement. Fearful parenting produces both passivity and legalism. Passive parenting can invite apathy or rebellion.

I (David) get to speak about the Axis message with caring adults all over the world. I will never forget an exchange I had with a mom at a Christian school. As I spoke about engaging your teen's world to better connect with their heart, I used a Taylor Swift song as an example. One mom in the crowd was visibly bothered. After the talk she pushed her way up to me with a surprising statement: "We are trying to raise our kids like the 1950s." I didn't know what to say.

She was so fierce for her kids. Her fear was unmistakable. She was a mama bear. You come between the mother bear and her cubs in the wilderness and you had better have an escape plan. Let's play this out.

What happens when trying to go back in a cultural time machine doesn't work? What happens when the fight you're putting up against culture shifts from loving your kid to hating everything they are exposed to? What happens when you feel like you lost that battle because you just couldn't keep holding your finger in the hole of the cultural dam? Where is that anger directed? What are you fighting against?

Misguided fear is running rampant in our culture. It pops up on Facebook or in blog comments or any place that offers people a voice. We're attached to our phones in part because we're swimming in fear. If we're not careful, we'll live in a state of continual cortisol bursts in the brain, constantly leaking anxiety. In those moments, we're separated from being present in the moment and loving our kids. We're distracted and dysregulated.

If you are a parent or a caring adult, you love this teen more than they'll ever know. You'd wrestle a mountain lion for them, just like mama bear from North Carolina. Your love bubbles into passion for your kids. That's amazing, but it easily becomes misguided passion.

It's natural. It's normal. It's good. It should be celebrated. But it becomes distracting, even destructive, when it's directed toward the wrong thing. When you think can control everything, or manipulate circumstances, you will accidentally end up hurting your kids and yourself in the process. You'll dismiss your child's growth and their journey into adulthood. You'll crowd their ability to make their own decisions.

Our team loves watching parents who are fierce for their kids. We think it's amazing that you can care for another human so much. We know you sacrifice for your kid. But we see the danger of this becoming misguided fear. So mama and papa bears (or grandpa, grandma, and mentor bears), keep loving these teens, but beware the danger of only loving them through your fear instead of through your connection to their heart.

How Will You React When You Find the Secret Box?

When Jeremiah and I were young, anything we wanted to hide from our parents got stashed in a box. They were physical things you could touch and look at hidden in some physical space. Now the secret box is digital. It's in a secret folder, app, or message thread parents likely won't find. In fact, there are apps (like a fake calculator app) that hide other things behind them. Remember, teens are smart and will find ways to get around things. We've got to give them some credit for this.

My wife and I (Jeremiah) were sitting in Wendy's eating a family dinner when my wife looked down to see one of our kids (who will remain nameless and genderless to protect their identity—wink, wink) quickly cover their phone screen. A sure sign of shadiness. We proceeded with our policy of accessing anything on "their" (technically "our") devices. As they scrolled through together, Kimberly saw a mention of an Instagram account in a text. The problem is they weren't allowed to have an Instagram account, but they had gone around the controls to create one. We let them sweat a little while they ate their junior bacon cheeseburgers.

As we drove home, we realized this was a crucial moment. We don't do everything right as parents, but we decided to take the high road on this one. When we got home, we had a real, meaningful, calm conversation about this and let them come clean. This moment served to build trust and wisdom.

How will you react when you uncover something on their phone, computer, or web history? When you uncover their secret stash (of anything), your reaction is important. I understand the fear, the disbelief, and the disappointment, but this can be a defining moment for your relationship. This happened to me (Jeremiah), and it has happened to many other parents.

Losing an Impossible Game

Do you ever feel like you're losing to culture? Between the mood swings, telling our kids no, not seeing eye to eye on hard issues, and keeping up with our fast-spinning culture, parenting can feel like a battle you're destined to lose. There are not many moments when we feel warm and fuzzy, like we're doing a half-decent job. The acceleration of culture based on the smartphone is alarming. When our team speaks to rooms full of parents, the conversations linger afterward. We've talked about it all with parents. You can't surprise us anymore.

We are experiencing unique issues today. A growing anxiety leading to increased suicide rates, the rise of pornography addiction, increased internet security issues, and the spiraling effects of social media are a few issues we'll discuss in depth later on. Those things deserve our attention and should be treated with care. They're real, but they don't tell the full story. Please don't focus solely on the timely issues; lift your eyes to the timeless solution. Jesus is life.

We've been given a timeless solution, to partner with Jesus. Every generation faces the timeless issues of sin, rebellion, and hiding and separation from God. The solution is written into the pages of the Old Testament. Yet we get to write the script with different handwriting. We were commissioned for it through Jesus' charge to go make disciples of all nations.

3

Your Wisdom, Their Wonder

If we get relationships wrong, little else matters.

Gabe Lyons and David Kinnaman[1]

Come to me, all you who are weary and burdened, and I will give you rest.

Jesus[2]

Our church believed the lie that they could outsource the spiritual development of our young people solely to me as the professional youth leader—perhaps because I never told them otherwise.

Kara Powell[3]

A small boy in sub-Saharan Africa walked into the room, afraid to interrupt his father from his important work. "Daddy, I have a question for you. When do you think it'll be my turn to die?"

Alarmed, his father said, "What makes you think that will happen?" The boy replied, "Well, Daddy, all my friends are dying." "You won't die of this," the father said confidently.

"How do you know?" the boy asked.

"Roll up your sleeves," the father said. "Those little scratches on your arm are called vaccinations. You got those in America before you came here so you wouldn't get these kinds of diseases."

The father's face went blurry, and the boy stammered, "Papa, that's not fair. Why don't all of my friends have scratches on their arms?" This was his first realization that the world was unfair and unequal. By the time he was fifteen, half his friends had died.

He would go to bed on his little cot listening to the drums of the funeral services stretch through most of the night and cry himself to sleep. A few days later it would be another one of his buddies. He just thought that's how it was; the young and the old were vulnerable. He figured that was the reality of life everywhere.

On his first day in the United States he stumbled into a grocery store to discover plenty of food, and into the drugstore to discover plenty of lifesaving vaccinations. He had an epiphany: There is plenty of food; none of his buddies needed to starve. There is plenty of medicine; none of them needed to die of diseases.

That is the story of Wess Stafford. He has served Compassion International for nearly half a century. Compassion serves two million kids a year who are in poverty. Much of his calling to release children in Jesus' name can be traced back to those early days of his childhood in Africa. When Wess shares his story across the world, he compares a child's spirit to wet cement just ready to be shaped by something or someone significant. Sometimes he "loses" the crowd for a moment as they scan back over their teenage years. He asks, "Who was it? What did they say to you? What did they do? Who believed in you before you believed in yourself?"[4]

No matter how old they are, your kids are taking in the culture around them. No matter what hard things they have experienced, God is shaping them for the rest of their lives, implanting justice and love and truth into them. They need you to help them shape and develop their story—the faith and dreams they will live out the rest of their lives. Perhaps the next president, justice advocate, or novelist eats dinner at your table every night.

Kids are being shaped far more than we imagine. They are soaking in their environment. They are being set up for a future, a calling, and a family. We need to attend to their hearts now. The role God has given you as a caring adult is massive, and we want to help. We want to equip you to shape your teen for lifelong faith during these moldable years.

Leaving the next generation alone to raise themselves or be raised by YouTube influencers or Instagram simply isn't an option. Wess Stafford says, "No one can say, 'Well, children are just not my thing—I don't "get" them. I don't know how to handle them, act around them, or relate to them.'"[5] Even if you don't have kids of your own, you can't just look the other way. The issues are real, but so is God's promise. The teen years are for preparation. Caring adults realize they are preparing their kids, or others they care about, for a jungle, not a zoo.[6] Life isn't lived in a cage or in a plastic environment. Parenting doesn't happen there either.

Jonathan Morrow says, "As our post-Christian culture increasingly marginalizes Christianity, it is critical for those of us who care about the next generation not to take a business-as-usual approach to their formation. If we do nothing, they will be shaped away from life with God in Christ. We have the opportunity to reimagine what passing on our faith to the next generation looks like in this unique cultural moment. Let's be creative, courageous, and faithful!"[7] It's going to take all three—creativity, courage, and faithfulness—to accomplish this.

Merging Wisdom and Wonder

The young have a gift. They see a vision of a world that doesn't exist. Life offers limitless possibilities waiting to be painted on an unending canvas. Skepticism hasn't yet shattered the window through which they are peering hopefully. Their view of reality is pure, and their vision is winsome and contagious. God gave youth the gift of wonder, but many teens are losing hope and losing vision. "The optimism of youth, it seems, has been warped into a crippling fear of failure," writes Rich Karlgaard.[8]

The old (or at least the older) also have a gift. Their experiences have informed them. They have fallen down, gotten up, course-corrected, and learned lessons. Ideally, they have collected information that has developed into a knowledge of how to live life well. Their steps are more calculated and informed. They have something to pass on to those who have lived fewer years. When we age well, we develop the gift of wisdom.

What if wisdom and wonder could fuse? What if the limitless wonder of teens could be tempered and grounded with the wisdom of adults?

Sometimes, as adults, we need to be shaken from our slumber and revived from our skepticism by the dreams of the young. Wisdom can make us play it safe, stop dreaming, and look past the sparks of new things God is doing. The wonder of teens can shape us and reawaken us to possibility, pulling our feet off the ground when our soles are stuck in the mud.

We need their wonder, and they need our wisdom. Their naïveté allows misplaced passion to bleed into shortsighted decisions. We can help them zoom out, prepare for the long haul, and make better decisions in light of the future. We can help them learn to live wisely. We believe God fashioned the wonder of teens to complement the wisdom of adults. This was his design.

There is a gap, sometimes a chasm, between the generations. The lines have been broken in most families, and wisdom and wonder are two islands with no life rafts between them. Parents and caring adults can bridge this gap. When the awkward and natural barriers of puberty and adolescence begin creating this chasm, parents can connect with the heart of their child.

The chasm only gets bigger if not connected early in the teen years. Now is the time. Your teen needs your wisdom, but they won't receive it if they don't trust you. You must connect with their heart. They must believe you are interested in their wonder too, not simply making a deposit of wisdom that "fixes" them. You desperately need doses of their wonder too.

Shouldn't the Church Be Discipling My Kids?

Pastors bear a lot of weight. They take on the hidden issues in the backstage of life that others don't see. They're often the first ones who get a call, text, or Facebook message in the middle of the night crying for help with the impending divorce, recent death, unfolding affair, or hopeless emergency. They are expected to show up for people in the good and the hard moments of life. Congregants have high expectations of pastors.

Student pastors today seem especially tired. They have been pulled to the center of social issues in youth culture such as chronic anxiety, suicide, cyber bullying, the effects of divorce, and the ubiquitous porn problem. Many parents want their help but don't know how to work together with them.

The blueprint has changed over the last thirty years. Student ministries cannot afford to simply be game-generating, fun-trip-planning, happy-go-lucky clubs like they were in the '90s and early 2000s. They are feeling the weight of working alongside schools and families on massive issues pressing youth culture. "Youth ministry is being forced to operate in a totally new context. The youth landscape is more complex, accelerated and diverse," concluded a recent study.[9] Student pastors are no longer cruise directors; they are missionaries in a foreign land and medics on a battlefield.

For various reasons, youth ministry has faced much criticism in the last decade, and this has been discouraging for many youth pastors and leaders. If you know a student pastor, family pastor, or campus minister who works with your kids, encourage them. Remind them that what they do matters. And disciple your own child. These leaders are willing to partner with you, but they want you to disciple your teen. Some parents of teens don't know Jesus. Some student pastors will adopt teens as their spiritual children, but bearing the sole weight of discipling teens is exhausting, and not their God-intended role.

In the history of the church, the role of full-time youth pastor is a recent development. Our Axis team is grateful for student pastors, not critical or skeptical of them. The rise of youth ministry has provided some great opportunities for students to deepen their faith, develop their leadership, cultivate a healthy social core around them, and walk more closely with caring adults. Perhaps as you read this, your mind wanders to mission trips, discipleship groups, and fun opportunities that shaped your own faith.

But there seems to be some dissonance between parents and student pastors. Here are some revealing stats from The Barna Group:

> 72% of parents expect the youth pastor to be discipling their teen.
>
> 34% of youth pastors believe there is a "lack of parent interest."[10]

Can you see the disconnect? Both sides have expectations that aren't being met. We recently met with a group of youth workers about their perspective on parents, and here is some of what they shared:

> In churches we basically have the same problem as your local school, very little involvement from parents.
>
> I'm torn on whether parents are helpful volunteers in student ministry, because when they are there students lose the freedom to ask their big questions.

Our parents have no expectation of partnership.

Eighty percent of our students are not from Christian homes.

Parents are intimidated. They don't know how to answer their kids' questions because they aren't growing themselves.

It is helpful to know what student pastors believe the issues are. Student pastors often serve as a helpful bridge between parents and students, but sometimes students get stuck on the bridge between the parent and the student pastor or older discipler.

There has been a lot of press in Christian circles the last few years about the staggering number of kids leaving the church as they become adults. Students are often connected to a student pastor, but are they connected to the church body? Has busyness made church one more commitment in an already cluttered and overwhelming schedule?[11] If you, as parents and caring adults, don't prioritize involvement in the church, why should we be surprised when they don't prioritize the church in their adulthood?

We have been intentionally working alongside student pastors, lead pastors, family pastors, and denominations to help them resource parents to disciple their kids. This is a crucial partnership for us. If you know a student pastor or leader discipling students, hand them this book when you're done with it or buy them a copy. And give them a high five from us while you're at it. We believe this can be both crucial to their understanding of parents as well as freeing to them.

Youth ministry has changed a lot in the last ten years. A youth pastor recently told our team, "Parents treat student ministry like the dry cleaners: Bring them to us, we'll clean them up, you pick them up when they're ready." Ouch! Naturally, we track along with the barriers, burdens, and developments student ministers are sensing. We recently asked a group of student pastors this question,

"What are the barriers to parents discipling their teens?" Here is what they said.

> They don't believe they are the most influential spiritual voice in their kid's life.
>
> They don't feel confident in their own knowledge about the Bible/faith.
>
> They say they are too busy.
>
> They are afraid.
>
> They don't have the tools.
>
> They take on a buddy mentality instead of a stewarding mentality.
>
> They lack intentionality.
>
> They believe discipleship is the church's responsibility. (This statement lines up with Barna's finding that about 3/4 of parents believe it is the church's responsibility to disciple their kids, so this naturally falls on the student pastor.)
>
> They don't feel they "have what it takes to disciple" their kid.
>
> They believe we are the experts.
>
> They often mix the word and process for "disciple and discipline," so they aren't actually teaching. "It's easier to scold than to teach or develop."
>
> Many of our students have parents who don't follow Jesus.
>
> We never see the parents, so it's hard to have a relationship with them.
>
> The rest of the church expects the youth to help with their thing, but no one turns back and invests in the students.

These statements may sound harsh, as though the student pastors are scolding parents or church staff teams, but the looks in their faces revealed care and exhaustion, not anger or frustration. They want to partner with parents, but they don't know how. There is a gap, a barrier, between most parents and most student ministries in churches.

When Helping Hurts

Tony is a father of three and serves on our Axis team. He is deeply passionate about discipleship. He has served the church in the United States and in Australia, and he has a unique perspective on this call to disciple the next generation. While he was reading the paradigm-shifting book *When Helping Hurts* and resonating with how we have addressed systemic issues of material poverty, he saw a connection. Here are Tony's thoughts.

> I was blindsided by a thought; we have done the same thing with the way we have addressed spiritual poverty.
>
> The authors unpack how we generally only offer relief to poverty situations. Solely offering relief in poverty only allows generational poverty to grow and doesn't actually help people move out of their current state. When we approach poverty, we should ask three questions:
>
> Does this need relief?
> Does this need rehabilitation?
> Does this need development?
>
> We have crippled the church by doing practically the same thing with spiritual growth. We simply offer relief. This has created a systemic issue of generational spiritual poverty that has led to spiritual atrophy. Most parents have no idea they have the spiritual muscle to disciple their children because it is in a state of atrophy. Remember the stat that 72% of parents believe it is the youth pastor's responsibility to disciple their children?[12]
>
> Somewhere along the way we lost sight of what God calls us to as parents in the Shema (Deuteronomy 6) and the Great Commission (Matthew 28). When Jesus commissioned us to make disciples, he didn't call us to merely preach the Good News. He didn't call

us into relief for the spiritually impoverished. Although that is an integral part, it is only the start. We must move beyond offering spiritual relief to begin spiritual rehabilitation and then move further to spiritual development.

Let's put it this way:

Relief = Jesus has rescued you from something.

Rehabilitation = Jesus has rescued you for something.

Development = Jesus has rescued you to join him in his redemptive work.

Many parents are stuck in relief work. They may know Jesus and acknowledge Jesus saved them, but they don't move beyond this. They haven't moved beyond some of their own generational spiritual poverty that was passed down to them. They don't realize God has placed them in their kid's life for a bigger purpose than bringing them into adulthood.

Some parents move beyond relief parenting into rehabilitation parenting. They realize they have a responsibility to pass on faith to their kids and be an example to them. They talk about Jesus and set an example their kids desperately need. But they stop just short of entering in at a heart level.

Fewer parents move into the posture of development. They take their call as spiritual guides for their kids seriously. They know it won't be easy, but it's worth it. They don't try to fix their kids, but they pray for them and seek to connect to the heart of their child. They start a lifelong run-on conversation toward faith that continues their entire life. They move in and out of how God's story intersects with their story. They talk about the beauty and the brokenness, the good and the ugly, the sin and the restoration. If you're reading this book, we believe you want this. You want to be a developer, not a just a reliever or a rehabber.[13]

We don't want your relationship and conversations to be shifting sand. We are supporting you in your role of helping your kids develop a lifelong faith. You can't do development work alone. We want to be part of your community. We want to help you live out your God-given calling to shape your child into a developed, mature disciple of Jesus.

You Don't Have to Know It All to Pass on Faith

We believe many parents deeply want to pass on faith to their kids, but they think they have to know all the answers to the questions their kids are asking. So, they consciously or subconsciously hide from hard conversations. Satan wants you to believe you don't have what it takes to shape this teen you love.

Teens aren't simply looking to be shaped in knowledge. A recent study revealed the top three things teens in thriving "vibrant" spiritual households desire from their parents: advice, sympathy, and encouragement.[14] This shouldn't surprise us; all three of those are heart connections that happen through the vehicle of conversation. And, of course, conversation is the way to the heart of teens.

The study goes on to conclude that parents get scared if they don't know the answers to their kid's questions. The good news is, "This does not mean we need to have all the answers—but it does mean that we need to create households where people feel safe to talk about and explore their doubts with the help of loved ones."[15]

It isn't simply about reading the Bible with your kids or conducting philosophy lectures at the dinner table (we don't recommend the lectures, by the way). So, what do vibrant families of faith do?

Share meals: Intentional meals are common in households that also carve out time for faith interactions.

Participate in spiritual conversations: This is a crucial element of their lives and families.

Pray and study the Bible: They intentionally read Scripture and pray together. Check out *The Bible Project* YouTube videos.

Spend time together and have fun: They carve out quality
time together and don't neglect the fun.

Practice hospitality: They create open space for those outside
of their family to be part of their household.[16]

The role of hospitality in developing lifelong faith is surprising.
It plays a major role in families with a thriving faith. Millennials
see this as a massive opportunity to express generosity, and households with a faith considered "vibrant" not only talk about faith,
pray, and study the Bible but also "welcome non-family visitors at
least several times a month."[17] Perhaps you not only need to have
conversations and meals with your teen, but also to invite others
around your table, into your home, and among your family.

Where Are All the Dads?

David and I both are dads, so we need to speak frankly. If the next
generation is going to develop into faith leaders, the dads are going
to have to show up big. The research indicates fathers play a smaller
role than mothers in terms of both presence and influence in their
households.[18]

I (Jeremiah) love the work of our partners at Restoration Project, as they seek to help fathers develop deeper relationship and
heart-level connection with their sons and daughters. In my case,
I have a lot of baggage from the past that gets in the way of loving my kids well. Restoration Project architects experiences that
lead men to better understand their own stories and heal their
own father-wounds in order to turn their hearts fully toward their
children.

I have had the opportunity to spend a weekend with each of
my kids individually. It was so life-changing for all of us, now I
send any friends I can to experience this with their children. We
highly recommend that every father who wants to intentionally
love his kids well attend.

From Restoration Project I learned some key categories that have been extremely helpful to me in understanding story— both my own and my children's. It's a glimpse at the greater meta-narrative of God's story in Scripture that we also see as life-shaping in each of our own micro-narratives we live here on earth.

Innocence: There are two meanings to the word *innocent*. First, and most commonly used, is "not guilty." We know from the fallen-ness of humanity that all have sinned, even our little ones. However, another meaning of innocent is "naive." When we are young and innocent, we are naive to the pain and struggle in the world until we experience it firsthand. All of us have a short window of innocence in our lives, when we have those sweet, tender, and uninhibited moments with our kids.

Tragedy: At some point, innocence is lost, and we become all too familiar with the pain and evil in the world. These tragedies may be a "capital T" tragedy such as a death, divorce, or experience of abuse. Far more common, however, are "little t" tragedies that accumulate over time, such as experiences of shame, guilt, harsh words, or being asked (mostly subtly) to take a twisted role in the family. Pain and the realities of the world shape the wound. And yes, it's normal and inevitable for mom and dad to unknowingly contribute to some of these lower-case traumas. While we may do our best, we still blow it.

These tragedies (both T and t) shape us as children and teach us how to survive in a broken and fallen world. This shaping impacts how we will relate to ourselves, God, and others.

Struggle: Every one of us wants to return to the innocence of the Garden. We know that we were not made for pain, but we also know life is full of it. Therefore, we struggle. Behind everyone's eyes is a secret story of tragedy, and we spend the bulk of our lives wrestling with our brokenness. From this place, a whole host of challenges emerges, such as addictions, depressions/anxieties, insecurities, confused identities, etc. For a parent, it is extremely painful to watch your child or teen wrestle through this pain and insecurity. The fact is, they will. And you do too.

This is why Restoration Project starts with the father. Far too often, when a parent does not heal these parts of their story, they will "leak" all over their children. Our stories as parents must be attended to or they will only grow and be transferred to the next generation.

As you read these words, perhaps your own struggle is real and palpable and was never addressed in your family. Do the work on behalf of your children. By watching you heal, they will learn they, too, have what it takes to walk through the struggle and come out victorious.

Restoration: Ultimately, true restoration comes with the fullness of the kingdom of God. Until then, we get to experience restoration in earth-bound ways. This is what we pray for in our children: God restoring the broken story lines in our kids. It's the place every human longs to be. It takes work and relationship and time to get there. It is a beautiful and redemptive place to be, where we can nurture and heal others. No one ends up here accidentally.

There is bad press out there about dads, but we see many dads doing fatherhood right. From camping trips with their kids to initiation rites of passage to praying for their kids to simply being present—it's possible to leave a spiritual legacy in your kids' lives. No dad is perfect, and we know it feels intimidating, but there are resources to help you both initiate your children into manhood and womanhood and to walk the journey alongside them.

Your children need both nurture and conversation to progress through these tumultuous transitions. They need you to enter into their story and lean in. They need hard questions and reassurances of love. They need to know you care. If your conversation is going to last somewhere around six decades, you need to start early. Begin now talking with your kids about the brokenness around them so they will let you into the tragedy, the struggle, and hopefully, the redemption. We know it's scary to enter into the pain, but it's more scary to think about leaving this unattended and passed on to future generations. Start the conversations now![19]

4

Conversation: The Hunger for WITH

Most conversations take at least seven minutes to really begin.

Andy Crouch paraphrasing Sherry Turkle[1]

Point your kids in the right direction—when they're old they won't be lost.

Proverbs 22:6 MESSAGE

The leader of the past may have been the person who knew how to tell, but certainly the leader of the future will be a person who knows how to ask.

Peter Drucker

It was devastating to become a statistic, especially for a couple who never thought they would find themselves struggling through divorce and watching their kids pick up the pieces. As you can imagine, their son and daughter were hurting. Their lives were rocked. Nobody wants their parents to not be together.

The daughter was left in the home, and she reached out to music to cope. Her biggest influence was Billie Eilish. Despite not wanting to listen to Eilish's music, her mom knew the words spoke to her daughter, and were where she felt like she belonged.

This mother chose to pursue a heart connection with her daughter over her own musical preferences. She entered her world and asked her questions about the words behind the music. She listened to her daughter's hurting heart and realized it wasn't about her. This mom chose conversation and connection. That is the heart of redemptive parenting. It's seeing God in the hard stuff. It's not about pretending; it's about engaging with the heart of your teen. We want to help you do that. Let's dig in.

Who's Actually Having Conversations?

Who's got two thumbs and is getting tired of social media war zones? Us! Just take one scroll through Facebook and you'll realize why people are jumping ship on social media: People aren't really talking anymore. What started as a space to converse and show others snippets of your life has become a space to prove your point and have knock-down-drag-out comment wars. It's one more stand someone is taking against another group, one more political post, one more offensive comment (they would never say to their face), one more article shared about why our world is a burning dumpster.

Everyone has a soapbox, and no one seems afraid to climb on it these days. Everyone is trying to be heard, but no one is convening conversations. Partially due to this toxicity, there is a deep hunger for conversation in our culture today. Your teen may not tell you this, but they want to have a conversation with you. They want to talk and be heard. But they're tired of being talked at and talked down to; they want to be talked with. Truth be told, we think everyone's tired of being told what to do. People are looking for healthy conversations to engage in, but they don't know how to find them.

Conversation Killers

We want you to cultivate a really long conversation with your kids. To foster that, it's helpful to identify some of the culprits that kill conversation.

Speed kills conversation. You know that feeling when you are running ten minutes late and someone wants to talk? You are rushing from one thing to the next, and they want to hold you back for a slow conversation. They obviously don't get the hint that you can't talk; it's all business right now!

Is that how you are around your teen? Are you too busy for conversation? Perhaps the frantic pace of life for your family is getting in the way of conversation. On average, conversations take around seven minutes to get rolling.[2] Parents of teens often comment, "My kids never want to talk when I want to talk, but as soon as I want to go to bed they're ready to talk!" It's a cruel joke. They seem to want to talk at the most inconvenient times. No one ever said intentional conversation was convenient.

Perhaps some of our busyness stems from viewing teenagers as a problem to solve, a task to complete, or an assignment to finish. Sharon Galgay Ketcham says, "The busyness of teenagers is connected to the longing of adults to help problematized teenagers make it into adulthood. Imagine if we saw teenagers as Christ does: full of potential to join God's purpose."[3]

Closed-mindedness kills conversation. When people don't want to know what the other person is thinking, it's not a conversation; it's a monologue. Curiosity shows care. A question shows dignity, because you genuinely care what the other person has to say. Be careful not to ask your teen questions that are really just statements with a question mark attached. You won't fool anyone, especially teens, by pretending you care when you honestly don't.

Due to divided politics, a general sense of polarization, and social media grenades, we have an increasing fear of conversation. A recent study concluded, "Less that one-quarter of American adults has a spiritual conversation once a month. More than half of people who claim no religion say they simply aren't interested in the topic. Concerns about coming off as angry, disrespectful or judgmental are main reasons people feel it can be inappropriate to discuss spiritual matters."[4] The bar for conversation and care in our culture is low. Really low.

Most conversations die before they ever start because we are too busy and closed-minded. God is about connection, and Satan loves disconnection. It makes sense that Satan is in the conversation-killing business, constantly keeping us busy and closed-minded so we don't invite others in. It also makes sense that these will be massive barriers to the one lifelong conversation you need to be moving in and out of with your kids.

Dads and Conversation

Dads, let's talk for a minute. We want to make an appeal to every dad reading this: Your teen needs conversation with you! The latest research shows that kids are more likely to have conversations with moms in major areas of life. Yay for moms; moms are awesome. Dads, please lean in here. A recent survey indicated your kids are more likely to have conversations with grandparents instead of you about all major areas they surveyed except for politics and sex (yeah, that one makes total sense—who wants to talk to granny about sex?!).[5]

Conversations with dads are lacking, and in many cases, non-existent. It makes sense that a majority of Gen Z said "their mom was the one who was there for them in their last personal crisis."[6] When you need comfort, you flee to whomever you are already connected to. Whoever is having the daily conversations with teens will be the one they come to when they are struggling, doubting, searching, or celebrating.

We think there's a bigger issue of spiritual and relational leadership at work in the family. Research also concluded, "Fathers do not seem to be filling either the role of logistical or spiritual leader as well as mothers."[7]

Moms seem to be holding family life together. Sure, there are factors that contribute to this. Perhaps this is due to proximity, busyness with work, or dads just not knowing how to have these conversations. We get it. We wrestle with these tensions every week also. But it's also easy to give excuses. These realities are sad and alarming.

Is it the chicken or the egg? Are dads' relationships with their kids flatlining because they lack conversation, or is conversation lacking because of flatlined relationships? Regardless of the cause, we need dads to step up and step in to begin and continue hard conversations about life and faith.

Dads, we have to start and continue this one conversation with our teens now! Most of us struggle a bit with the sit-and-talk thing, so we might need to take a different angle. Take your daughters on dates (even when they're teenagers). You can always bring your teen along on the things you're already doing (like a business trip), but look for things they want to do and join them. Here are some conversation catalysts to get the talking started.

Conversation Catalysts

Doing things together. It's often easier for men to converse shoulder-to-shoulder instead of face-to-face. In other words, we like to do stuff together. So take your kids camping. Eat meals you both love. Go bowling. Stuff your kids full of ice cream. Take them to the concert they want to go to. Build something together. Take a fun weekend away. We don't care what you do, just spend time and find a way to talk!

Asking good questions. Questions actually call teens into maturity. They get the opportunity to share their perspective. Even if you don't agree with them, just listen. Keep it rolling! Ask another question. Invite them to share a deeper perspective. Let them sit with their answer a bit. Often teens have never had the chance to vocalize their perspective to an adult. Remember, the goal of a conversation isn't to come to a consensus but to learn what your teen is processing and to show them you care.

For a long time leaders have known that the Socratic method, in which you lead and guide by asking questions, is highly effective. There are coaches today in nearly every field leading by asking questions. Step into a courtroom and listen to lawyers lead the whole room toward an understanding of who is guilty simply based on asking the right questions. Counselors and therapists lead toward healing by asking intelligent questions. Consultants lead businesses to cross barriers and gain productivity by discerning the right questions to ask. Questions are engaging and offer dignity. They pave the way for maturity and paradigm shifts.

The activity or the content of the conversation isn't the main thing; a heart connection with your teen is. Don't wait until a crisis arises to try to cultivate conversation. Start after school today. Block off Saturday to do something fun. Find common activities and drift into conversation. As with anything new, it may be awkward at first, but it's worth it.

Don't forget that those hard, weird, or painful situations can be great conversation catalysts. In our (Jeremiah's) basement we found one of our kids doing a strange YouTube challenge under a sibling's bed when he was supposed to be off screens. We had to have conversations about not secretly building toilet-paper forts at the grocery store (our kids actually tried this because one of the YouTube channels they watch showed young people building such forts at grocery stores, usually without the permission of store owners, and said YouTube stars did not teach the impressionable kids watching, i.e., my kids, that this might be frowned upon by the management or the authorities). I sure didn't learn to do this watching *America's Funniest Home Videos* when I was a kid. We've had painful discipline turn into deeper relationship. If you're intentional about this, you can have small or big redemptive conversations that bring you closer.

Here's the point: Do things *with* your kids. Fight the urge to be on different screens in different rooms. Talk with them about why that was a dumb decision instead of yelling at them. Take them along on a business trip whenever possible. Bring them along on a cool opportunity. Let them pick the dinner place. Let them join you and your friends on that guys' or girls' trip when they're old enough. You're depositing relational equity into their account that they'll be living off the rest of their lives. The best things in life are done with others.

5

Translating Culture

Take your Bible and take your newspaper, and read both. But interpret newspapers from your Bible.

Karl Barth

In an increasingly diverse and religiously pluralistic culture, we cannot settle for teenagers to become the same kinds of conversation-challenged disciples. The gospel compels us to be conversation-enabled.

The Barna Group[1]

A house is built by wisdom and becomes strong through good sense. Through knowledge its rooms are filled with all sorts of precious riches and valuables.

Proverbs 24:3–4 NLT

Before drifting off to sleep at home or in the back seat on a long car ride, I (Jeremiah) was pulled into stories. Siblings slipped into a foreign land with beauty, temptation, brokenness, and a bigger story.

C. S. Lewis was shaping me through his stories of a lion, a witch, and a wardrobe, inviting me to a secret land. Lewis was translating a timeless Gospel into beautiful and timely stories that pulled me in. There was a bigger story he was translating into my life.

We desperately need to be translating both our culture and the Gospel into the hearts, minds, and imagination of kids. We need leaders who will do the work to stoke the imagination and to learn to be fluent in our culture with the timeless backdrop of the Gospel. Jesus is in the restoration business. Lewis was always translating culture and synthesizing it with the Gospel. Thinkers like Francis Schaeffer, John Stonestreet, and teachers at Summit Ministries helped me understand how faith, culture, and social issues intersect.

In his classic *The Weight of Glory*, Lewis writes, "It would seem that our Lord finds our desires not too strong, but too weak. We are half-hearted creatures, fooling about with drink and sex and ambition when infinite joy is offered us, like an ignorant child who wants to go on making mud pies in a slum because he cannot imagine what is meant by the offer of a holiday at the sea. We are far too easily pleased."[2] How relevant this is today. We have been pulled into the shallows of dabbling in entertainment, addiction, boredom, and a codependent relationship with technology, and have lost sight of our Father.

We often say that if C. S. Lewis and Snapchat had a baby it would be named Axis. We're only half joking. We continue to take the most current and the most timeless and mix them together so the Gospel can be clear and approachable. We are known as culture translators, and this is also the name of our weekly dispatch on youth culture that goes out to tens of thousands of parents and teen influencers. We want to put our money (and energy) where our mouth is.

What Is Culture Translation?

To understand culture translation, we first need to define our terms. So what exactly is *culture*? How would you define it? Honestly, it's hard to define because it's so powerful and entrenched in our lives, yet nebulous and immeasurable.

Philosopher John F. Kavanaugh defines culture as "a cult . . . a revelation system" that "quietly converts, elicits commitments, transforms, provides heroics, suggests human fulfillments. Culture . . . is a gospel—a book of revelation—mediating beliefs, revealing us to ourselves."[3] He goes on to declare that "although culture is *made* by humans, it in a special manner makes us—to some extent in its own image."[4] His choice of terms is important; most of us are gleefully unaware of just how much our culture shapes what we think, what we believe, and how we perceive reality. Our cultural context even shapes how we interpret Scripture and our very faith in Christ. We tend to make God in our cultural image even though we often don't realize it.

Next, we need to understand a more familiar term, *cultural literacy*. E. D. Hirsch refers to cultural literacy as the ability to understand and participate fluently in a given culture.[5] Just as one can become literate in a language or economics or politics, one can also become literate in one or many cultures. *Culture translation* builds on this concept. Here's how we define it:

Culture translation: the ability to understand, participate fluently in, engage, and transform a given culture.

Knowing enough to participate fluently in a culture is good, but having the desire and ability to challenge a culture and call it to a higher standard is even better. Culture translation is all about generational cultures. Just as someone from China can feel totally lost and confused when visiting Mexico, someone from one generation can feel totally lost and confused around someone from another generation living in their own home. Sound familiar?

Their experiences, backgrounds, values, ideals, and even language can be so completely different that it's hard for them to relate to or understand each other, despite being raised in the same country. Yes, even though people from two generations might technically speak the same language, they often don't understand each other because their words and dialects (and emojis) are totally different.

Imagine sixty-something grandparents visiting their teenaged grandkids. The grandkids are talking about V-bucks and emotes, whether they saw someone's "story," who's DMed whom, that crazy "meme," and so on. Though these terms and ideas are part of the grandkids' everyday verbiage and experience, the grandparents typically have no idea what they're talking about. And because of this gap of understanding, it's hard for either generation to communicate—let alone connect—with each other. So much is lost in translation.

Why Do We Need Culture Translation?

Through studying different generations and cultures, those who engage in culture translation not only understand others better, they can also communicate effectively with them about things that matter because they understand what motivates them and how to speak their language. More important, it's a crucial component of faith. When we say that to parents, they often look at us and say, "The Gospel is all we need. Why are you trying to add to it?" A valid question.

Culture translation is not changing, adding to, watering down, or ignoring parts of the Gospel; it's simply changing the ways in which we communicate the Gospel and show its relevance to teens' lives. It's an awareness of how new generations communicate, what they're influenced by, and what they like. That awareness informs how we communicate the Gospel to them and shows how it's much more fulfilling than anything else they're into.

We didn't invent culture translation. In fact, we modeled it after what we observed in Scripture. During Jesus' time, the Jews lamented the pantheistic, hedonistic Roman culture in which they lived. They could see how at odds it was with their efforts to follow God and his laws. They longed for the day when their prophesied Messiah would come and restore things to the way they were supposed to be. In the meantime, they had to figure out how to live out their faith in the real world, but how to do that was another dilemma.

Jesus as Culture Translator

In Scripture, we see three main ways in which devout Jews sought to engage a hostile culture and live out their faith in God in a world that rejected him.

Isolation. First were the isolationists (the Essenes), who chose to run away from Roman culture and start their own counterculture, literally out in the desert.

Revolution. Second, we see the violent revolutionaries (the Sicarii) who took the opposite approach, physically rebelling against Roman rule in their efforts to establish the Kingdom of God on earth.

Integration. Third were those who said, "If you can't beat Rome, you might as well join 'em" (the Sadducees and Herodians), colluding with their Roman overlords to gain power and prestige.

So which approach to culture did Jesus choose when he launched his ministry? His own. Rather than running away from, colluding with, or even waging war against culture, he engaged with it in order to redeem it. He studied it, learned the language, customs, rituals, beliefs, and religions of his day. You guessed it: Jesus is our model for engaging your teen's world in order to see them transformed.

When he started his ministry, Jesus didn't start an isolated community or a violent rebellion. He didn't even try to change Roman laws to be more in favor of the Gospel he was teaching. Instead, he gathered twelve men and several women around him to teach and disciple as he went from place to place, interacting with both

Greeks and Jews and offering them a new, alternative way of life within the Roman culture. He talked about a new kingdom, but it wasn't a kingdom of this world. We need to reclaim his posture of engagement.

He chose to be a force of transformation from within by understanding, participating in, and engaging the culture. Jesus engaged culture by how he lived his life and conducted his ministry. He also engaged through his words. He spoke in parables, using words that were familiar to his audience: *harvest*, *wineskins*, *mustard seed*, *oil lamps*, *fig trees*, and being *fishers of men* (all things that need be explained to modern-day readers). The parable of the rich man (recorded in Mark 10:17–31, also in Matthew 19 and Luke 18) includes the statement: "It is easier for a camel to go through the eye of a needle than for someone who is rich to enter the kingdom of God." Jesus didn't invent that aphorism; it was a well-known phrase from the Babylonian Talmud. The original phrase was about an elephant, not a camel. But Jesus knew that his Palestinian audience had never seen an elephant, so he "translated" the idea by changing it to the biggest creature they knew so that it made more sense to them.

Paul as Culture Translator

Paul was also a master translator of culture. As a Roman citizen and a Pharisee, he expertly understood both Romans and Jews. Acts 17:16–34 gives us a clear example of how he wielded this knowledge to the Gospel's advantage. Paul had been traveling to different cities and preaching the Gospel in synagogues to Jews. Some of the Jews didn't like his message, so his followers became afraid for his life and sent him to Athens. And that's where we pick up the story.

While Paul was waiting for them in Athens, he was greatly distressed to see the city was full of idols. So he reasoned in the synagogue with both Jews and God-fearing Greeks, as well as in the marketplace day by day with those who happened to be there. A group of Epicurean and Stoic philosophers began to debate with him. Some of them asked, "What is this babbler trying to say?" Others remarked, "He seems to be advocating foreign gods." They said this because Paul was preaching the Good News about Jesus and the Resurrection.

Notice how Paul becomes "greatly distressed" because of his observations. He was in a new place, observing a new culture. And because he was paying attention, he noticed the idols. But we love his reaction! Instead of writing them off or going to his followers and telling them how sinful these people were, he engages. He goes to the synagogue, not to yell at them, but to reason with them. He also engages in the marketplace—where the non-Jews would be—with anyone who's willing to listen. And by doing that, he's overheard by the philosophers from two of the predominant schools of thought in Roman culture.

He debates with them. This means he already understood their philosophies. Then they took him and brought him to a meeting of the Areopagus, where they said to him, "May we know what this new teaching is that you are presenting? You are bringing some strange ideas to our ears, and we would like to know what they mean." (The Athenians and the foreigners who lived there spent their time doing nothing but talking about and listening to the latest ideas.) Paul was not only being winsome, but also employing reason and logic, so these pagans were intrigued and wanted to hear more. They invited him to their turf, the Areopagus.

They invited Paul to address them: He stood up in the assembly and said: "People of Athens! I see that in every way you are very religious. For as I walked around and looked carefully at your objects of worship, I even found an altar with this inscription: to an unknown god. So you are ignorant of the very thing you worship—and this is what I am going to proclaim to you" (Acts 17:22–23). Then he launches into a beautiful explanation of God and who God really is.

There are two things of note in his explanation:

1. He understood their culture, but instead of being offended by what he learned, he used it to begin a discussion to point them back to God.
2. He knew God so well that he could translate him in a compelling way to both Jews and Athenians. We know it was compelling because of how the story ends: When they heard about the resurrection of the dead, some of them sneered, but others wanted to hear more. Their curiosity was stoked.

It was powerful and drew them in. After that moment some became followers of Paul and believed. Many wanted to continue the discussion, while others were convinced enough to believe.

We love this story. It reveals Paul's ability to study, comprehend, and translate Athenian culture. He spoke in terms and symbols that different audiences understood. It showcases his depth of knowledge of God and how to speak about him in a winsome way to different audiences. Many others also translated culture throughout Scripture. As you read your Bible, they'll pop out to you. We can engage with Scripture and people closely enough to invite them into a beautiful picture of the Kingdom of God.

Culture translation is an art, not a science. It's not a formula. It's a messy picture that requires practice, finesse, and adaptation. We're dealing with humans—unique, unpredictable, ever-changing humans. If you're a parent or grandparent, you already know that doing the exact same thing with all of your children and grandchildren doesn't work. You need to know their personalities, quirks, and insecurities and adapt for them. Your kids are unique. So are their experiences, personalities, and responses.

Now it's your turn for culture translation. Head over to Billboard's Hot 100 chart and choose one of the top ten most popular songs. Choose a song or artist you've heard or your teen listens to. Listen to it and find the music video. (Heads up, many music videos are inappropriate, so we're not responsible.) Now analyze it. Write down your thoughts and reactions. We'll come back to them later. Once you've done that, you'll use this same song to walk through the steps below.

The Process of Culture Translation

Pray. Maybe this is obvious, but it's really important. As we look into culture, which is often loaded with depravity, it will affect us. We invite God to protect our hearts and minds, give us discernment, and help us know what to pursue and what to release.

Ask questions. This is how we discover what to research. We do this by asking general questions. What songs are popular right now? What's trending on social media? What movies are releasing soon? What TV shows are teens watching? Or even better, we ask our teens themselves. It may feel awkward, but instead of guessing, why not just ask them? Make sure to emphasize you're just curious, and don't analyze or judge. This is just fact-finding. Hold on for the rest.

Research. Now that you have a few cultural artifacts, it's time for research. Find out as much as you can about it. Collect sufficient information about the artifact so you can better understand it. When researching a song, movie, or show, find out how popular it was on the charts, how much money it's made, how many streams it has, and what social media accounts are attached to it. Now listen to it or watch it. For a celebrity or online influencer, find their social media presence, scroll their posts, and watch some of their videos. For an app, do some research, then download it and use it a bit.

It's tempting to read one Christian review and base all our conclusions on that, without ever experiencing the artifact ourselves. But this isn't fair and often misses many other valid viewpoints. Be purposeful in choosing reviews from both Christian and non-

Christian sources, as well as from older writers and younger ones. If we never read what Millennials and Gen Zers say (regardless of how wrong they might be), we're missing the point of understanding why our teens like that thing. And if we never actually consume the media, how can we understand its appeal? For your final step, compare notes with other parents, teachers, or pastors.

Analyze. Once you've gathered the info, it's time for analysis. Start on the surface: What was your visceral response to it? What did it look or sound like? What do you feel? Think? Want? How does it influence or move you? This is where we really have to put ourselves in our kids' shoes and imagine how they experience the artifact in question. We may have strong filters that help us recognize lies or get us to question the motive behind things, but our teens may not have those yet. They may simply experience without taking time to ask good questions or analyze it. You'll notice things that are more subliminal or less obvious.

Here are some filters to use:

What's good? It's important to start by noticing the good in something, even if it's overwhelmed by bad. This could be that "it's catchy," "it's well filmed," "it's entertaining." When we start with the good, we give our kids the benefit of the doubt and break down walls.

What's wrong? Now we can point out what's jacked up in the artifact.

What's missing? Often something important is left out.

What's confused? Something may be twisted or distorted. Reveal how it misses the mark.

What does Scripture say? We love this part even though it can be a hard step. The Bible doesn't mention Fortnite, Snapchat, or the latest meme, but how does it apply? Explore underlying ideas and principles, then see how the Bible addresses those. Social media, for example, isn't in the pages of Scripture, but it does speak to our need for validation, community, connection, and true identity. So, what does God's Word say about those things?

Discuss. Now we take what we've learned and talk about it with our kids. It's crucial not to lecture them or hammer them with truth! Focus on conversations, not monologues. We can do this by utilizing the Socratic method (question asking) to foster critical thinking. Pose questions that invite them to think logically and critically and come to a balanced conclusion. Use the filter questions above to get them thinking. Remember, the goal is to train their consciences, not be their conscience for them. It's often more powerful to guide them to the truth, rather than spoon-feed it to them.

Pray. We close with prayer, just as we opened. We need Christ now more than ever! Thank him for the opportunity to engage in your teen's world, for discernment, and for being bigger than culture. Ask him to protect your teen's heart and give you faith greater than your fears. Ask for more opportunities to talk about what matters to your kids.

Let's go back to the song you chose earlier. Apply these six steps to the track, writing down your answers to the five questions.

What did you discover about it? How was the analysis using the six steps of culture translation different from your prior analysis? What did you learn?

Songs are the easiest cultural artifacts to analyze, but you can apply this method to any cultural artifact: music, artists, celebrities, video games, social media influencers, movies, TV shows, sports, awards shows, apps, slang, memes, devices, social media. If it's part of culture, it can (and should) be analyzed.

Your posture of engaging is crucial. For culture translation to be effective, remain humble, kind, and curious. Arrogance and judgment are quick turnoffs. As hard as it might be, try to hold back your over-care. The older your kids get, the more autonomy they need. In order for them to become more responsible, they need trust. Otherwise they'll secretly rebel and hide stuff from you. They are becoming more responsible for their own lives and choices, and we want them to think for themselves. We need to rely on the Holy Spirit to work in our kids' lives in his timing.

What if your posture was more like that of a bartender (or barista) instead of a professor? A bartender sits and listens, asking questions but never getting too emotionally involved. For many, having a listening ear is so helpful that they talk their way through their problems without the bartender having to utter a word. On the other hand, a stereotypical arrogant professor stands above "intellectual inferiors" imparting immense knowledge. Questions are a nuisance to professors, and their students need to just shut up and listen, even if what the professor is talking about is irrelevant or useless to them. It's obvious which of these would be most inviting and helpful to our kids. Listen, ask questions, and encourage them as they work through ideas and problems. Feel free to add junk food to the equation for improved results.

Sometimes we confront depravity head on. It will be discouraging, frustrating, confounding, and disheartening. Trust us, we get it. When we study teen culture, we stare depravity in the eyeballs. Ignorance is not bliss; it is walking away from faithful engagement with our teens. We also need to keep our eyes and hearts from solely focusing on the ugliness of the world. We need to keep our eyes peeled for beauty.

Spying for Beauty

Dostoyevsky has inspired readers for centuries with his idea that beauty will be the thing that saves the world. As far back as Plato, beauty was understood not merely as an adornment or something in the eye of the beholder, but as a value judgment—a value just as important as truth and goodness. In many ways, beauty functions sacramentally: It bears the divine through the ordinary. When we encounter something beautiful, it should feel transcendent. We should feel like we've just experienced a taste of God.

Our modern world has severed the relationship between beauty and the divine. And in so doing, anything can pass as beautiful. When we turn our back on beauty, we become increasingly surrounded by ugliness. In pop culture, the question is no longer, "Is this beautiful?" but rather "Will it make money?" Sounds a lot like prostitution. We live in the age of pragmatism, where the values of cost and function trump beauty.

Think about architecture for a minute. At one time architecture beautified shared spaces, but now we build for cost and utility. Think about your home or your neighborhood. Is it truly beautiful? Or is it solely functional? Is it possible that Christianity can be communicated through the lens of beauty?

In his book *Beauty Will Save the World: Rediscovering the Allure & Mystery of Christianity*, Brian Zahnd writes,

> To a skeptical world we are generally more accustomed to defend Christianity in terms of its truth and goodness. But beauty also belongs to the Christian faith. And beauty has a way of sneaking past defenses and speaking in unique ways. To a generation suspicious of truth claims and unconvinced by moral or ethical assertions, beauty has a surprising allure. . . . A Christianity that is deeply enchanted by Christ's beauty . . . has the opportunity to present to a skeptical and jaded world an aspect of the gospel that has been too rare for far too long. Where truth and goodness fail to win an audience, beauty may once again captivate and draw those it enchants in the kingdom of saving grace. . . .
>
> Our task is not to protest the world into a certain moral conformity, but to attract the world to the saving beauty of Christ. We do this best . . . by enacting a beautiful presence within the world.[6]

God is the author and creator of both truth and beauty, so anywhere we find truth or beauty, no matter how surrounded by falsehood and/or ugliness, it's still God's truth and God's beauty. And beauty is part of the argument, part of what makes something compelling. Even though most artifacts in pop culture are full of terrible ideas, they're often very well made and beautiful—which is why so many teenagers continue to engage with them. Think about this: If all we ever do is point out what's wrong with culture and what's bad about what teens are immersed in, is this winsome? They'll begin to think God is only against things and people, not for them. Studies conducted for the book *UnChristian* revealed Christians are already known as nay-sayers, doomsday-ers, and haters, not people looking for beauty.

What if we began pointing out the good things? Can we point out beauty and truth as signposts toward God and his Kingdom? Then teens could better discern what God is for, rather than just what he's against.

The story of Jesus' life, death, and resurrection is not only the greatest story ever told, it's also the most beautiful story ever told. Beauty is graceful and has a way of sneaking past our defenses. It's hard to argue with beauty. It's powerful, much more powerful than sin and depravity and hopelessness, just as Anne Frank wrote in *The Diary of a Young Girl*: "I don't think then of all the misery, but of the beauty that still remains."[7]

Here are some helpful questions to point out beauty around us. How am I cultivating beauty in my home? How do you know if and when something is beautiful? How do I teach my kids to discern beauty from brokenness?

6

Missionaries Cleverly Disguised as Parents

You are only as sick as your secrets.

Alcoholics Anonymous adage

I cannot answer the question, "What ought I to do?" unless I first answer the question, "Of which story am I a part?"

Alasdair MacIntyre[1]

Whatever we do, we must not treat the Great Commission like it's the Great Suggestion.

Charles Swindoll

A father of two and friend of Axis has been on a crazy adventure with his kids. He never thought he would be a single dad. Suddenly he found himself doing things on his own—laundry, cooking, shopping, giving advice about boys and girls. When mom stepped out of the picture, it was really difficult for the kids. The kids struggled, but they really rallied. It was surprising the resilience that they showed in accepting a new normal and a new way of life.

They all learned on the fly. It was not a smooth process all the time. One day the daughter told her father she wanted to live life as a boy and she wanted to be referred to with "he," "him," and "his" pronouns. Everything in him thought, "Let's not go down that path!" He knew that the life of a trans person is difficult. They're more likely to self-harm, they're more likely to commit suicide, they're even more likely to be murdered. And that's a scary thing for a parent. No parent dreams of their kid walking that path.

Social media had been a big influence as she transitioned. She wouldn't have known much about what it looked like to be a trans person before she got involved in Tumblr. That opened up a world to her and took her down that path. How devastating to have your child affirmed in that behavior.

He began to discover conversation with his kids fueled by our parent guides. He learned more about what was swirling around his kids and became more informed about what to talk about and the biblical perspective behind that. He talked thoughtfully about social media, culture, fashion, movies, and whatever else came up.

As his youngest daughter got her learner's permit, he saw an opportunity: many hours together in the car. They talked about everything from K-pop bands to college to gender and sexuality to you name it. They redeemed time that he previously would have seen as a waste. He wouldn't trade those hours in the car for anything. That was a forced opportunity for them to sit and listen to each other.

Getting conversations going and being able to talk to his kids and keep the channels of communication open was so critical for their family. He's playing the long game. He's not thrilled about everything in his kids' lives, but he is setting up for the next thirty or forty years of conversation and relationship.

Instead of living out of a spirit of fear, he is choosing to embrace the excitement and encouragement around what's going to come for them. They know they've got a dad who's in their corner. The complexities of this story are unimaginable for many parents. But we love playing a part in crucial conversations behind the wheel of a car or around a dinner table.

Your Opportunity and Your Responsibility

Here is what we wholeheartedly believe: Parents and grandparents are the most efficient missionary model in the universe. You are God's plan for growing your kids up in the faith. We know you might feel like you're not (fill in the blank) enough to develop your kid. We can all insert our own insecurity in the blank: *cool* enough, *young* enough, *old* enough, *wise* enough, *spiritual* enough, *prepared* enough, *theological* enough. Parents, whatever you feel like you are not enough of, you are God's plan to shape your teen.

Please be bold! On the whole, the discipleship plan of the last thirty years where we just take kids to events to learn about Jesus hasn't developed a deep spiritual maturity. As we shared earlier, we are big fans of the church and those in the church who serve and disciple students. But a student pastor or youth worker was never meant to carry the weight of discipleship like a parent is. Thank anyone who influences your teen toward Jesus, but realize they are a supplement to how you are discipling your kid.

Thinking that a youth worker is the primary spiritual influence on your kid is like putting a third-string point guard into the NBA finals. We need a whole team, and they make each other better all season long, but the finals aren't the time to pull the guy from the end of the bench. It's your turn to get the ball down the court.

A former student pastor shared with us that one of his greatest struggles was getting the parents to understand they had the primary spiritual responsibility in their kids' lives, not him. They would gather monthly with other youth workers, and every person in the room was feeling the same frustration. Many of these youth workers did not have kids yet and couldn't understand the fears and overwhelmed state of parents. Instead of shaming parents for not taking responsibility, they made a commitment to clearly express to parents, "*You* are the primary influence on your child's spiritual growth, but we are here to reinforce." It was freeing to remind parents of this biblical invitation and mandate in Deuteronomy chapter 6. Youth pastors still have a crucial role in helping students and parents view cultural issues through the lens of the Gospel.

The Rituals in Your House

There is a liturgy unfolding in every home. It shapes us in deep and profound ways we don't even see, and we won't experience the effects for years. Christian thinker James K. A. Smith writes, "The household is also a deeply formative (or *de*formative) space that teaches us how to love from infancy. We love because he first loved us, but we learn *how* to love at home."[2] Have you thought about the liturgy of your family before? It's crucial.

No one would argue that what we practice in worship with our churches matters. It shapes families of faith and has divided families of faith over the centuries. Smith goes on to say, "So if we need to be intentional about the liturgies of Christian worship in the congregation, we should be equally intentional about the liturgies of the household."[3] If the adage "more is caught than taught" holds any water, we must take an audit of our family rituals.

Your family rituals reveal your family values, and they will shape family behavior. Smith reminds us, "You could have Bible 'inputs' every day and yet still have a household whose frantic rhythms are humming along with the consumerist myth of production and consumption. You might have Bible verses on the wall in every room of the house and yet the unspoken rituals reinforce self-centeredness rather than sacrifice."[4] The goal is not simply to possess knowledge about God, although that is good, but to have a relationship with God, to know him. I bet you want your kids to have a lifelong faith, not just stored-up knowledge.

We want to cast a vision and support your path toward redemptive parenting. We want to hear more stories of parents who choose to engage culture en route to the Gospel, even amidst painful and messy situations. Every parent wants good things for their children. We believe God wired that impulse into parents to show the love and goodness of God. Remember Jesus' words: "You fathers—if your children ask for a fish, do you give them a snake instead? Or if they ask for an egg, do you give them a scorpion? Of course not! So if you sinful people know how to give good gifts to your children, how much more will your heavenly Father give the Holy Spirit to those who ask him" (Luke 11:11–13 NLT).

Parents who choose a third way choose the redemptive path. They have seen the goodness of God and have received the invitation to walk the path of freedom through Jesus' life, death, and resurrection. Is that easy? No. Will we be perfect at it? Of course not. A life of faith and freedom is worth the investment required to pass it on. Third-way parents are in the trenches, having the hard conversations and pushing through shame and self-doubt. They realize there is a path other than drowning in the fears that can easily grab us or sticking our head in the sand and pretending we're living in easy times. There's middle ground.

We believe parents can live as redemptive agents of God's kingdom to their kids. And many are. Those parents are our heroes.

SECTION 2

HOW TO ENGAGE WITH YOUR TEEN

7

Cultivating a Heart Connection

Our lives begin to end the day we become silent about things that matter.

Martin Luther King Jr.

Don't aim for perfection. Aim for progress. Learn to slow the process down when your adrenaline gets pumping.

Crucial Conversations

Loneliness is proof that your innate search for connection is intact.

Martha Beck[1]

As my (Jeremiah's) son approached twelve, I was voraciously reading anything I could get my hands on about developing a boy into a man. As I planned and prepared to welcome him into manhood, I felt the resistance; it was harder than I imagined and it hadn't even started yet. Every resource talked about the importance of rites of passage.

On his twelfth birthday my wife took him out to a restaurant he loved and had a conversation about things that would be changing in their relationship. I met them there, we gave him some gifts, and then I took him to the next stop to explain the details of "Man Year" to him. I invited a handful of men, including David, to speak wisdom into his life. That year I watched some movies with him that had redemptive themes relating to manhood. Everything built toward a project he was deeply interested in: making a film. We decided to go above and beyond and rented out a movie theater for the premier and invited friends and family. Why not?

The year culminated with his thirteenth birthday party with friends at our home celebrating him and the mentor men who had spoken into his journey offering him a blessing him with their words. He noticeably changed and matured through that process. When you spend that much intentional time with a boy, then tell him "you are now a man," something changes.

There are no perfect parents, but there are intentional ones. If you want a heart connection with your kid, you are going to have to be intentional. You may not plan "Man Year" for your son or take your daughter across the country, but you can find little ways to be intentional building a relationship with them. Up to this point we've shared much about why one conversation with the teen you love can change everything. We've discussed who kids are and what they are looking for from their parent. We've addressed how you take the posture of a caring adult who is for them and not actively opposed to the culture they are immersed in.

Now we are going to lead you through how to do just that. This is a practical chapter. View this as a path; follow this process and you can shape your conversation with your teen for years to come. We have some exercises for you in this chapter, so slow down your pace and take some time to journey through this. It may be the most practical experience we leave you with in the whole book. Let's dig in to the four levels of conversation.

Level-One Conversations: Awareness of Your Approach

Before you crack open conversations with your teen, you need to know that the aim isn't perfection, it's progress. If you haven't begun your one conversation yet, now is your time. As a caring adult, sometimes you'll feel disrespected by the teen you love, you'll get angry, and you won't think clearly. Enter conversations with an open mind, loving heart, and steady pulse.

We realize it feels like anything new your teen is doing can feel like an emergency. You probably don't understand this new app, habit, or flavor of the week they're into. The flood of things coming at your kid is never-ending, and the easiest thing to do is give up the battle of trying to track their new interests. What if instead of viewing any new thing as an emergency you viewed it as an opportunity for conversation? Would that change things?

No one has more passion or care for your teen than you do. But your love for your teen (and the fear that naturally results) can turn nearly anything into a perceived emergency. It's important to know the difference between an emergency, when your teen is in danger, and a perceived emergency, when there is something you need more clarity on.

Exercise: Take five minutes and write down three to four emergencies happening right now with your teen. Decide whether they are actual emergencies or just perceived emergencies.

If everything is an emergency, your relationship will be drenched in fear. Your teen won't feel safe with you and will conceal things from you, so you don't know what is actually going on in their life. Without safety, how will you ever connect with the heart of your teen and see real change? In our experience, the parents who connect most with their teen are not the ones who talk the most or know the most. They're the ones who have built trust over many years.

Exercise: Take a moment to evaluate your relationship with your child. Rate your trust level from one to ten. Why did you land on that number? Identify a situation you want to address with your teen right now. Decide if it is necessary and worth bringing up right now. If you approached the conversation now, would it be proactive and out of care, or reactive and out of fear or anger?

Our team deals with so many parents who not only see everything as an emergency, but also see no way to parent other than how they were raised. We get it; parenting can be scary and frustrating. Perhaps you didn't learn this from your parents. Maybe fear, guilt, and shame were the only tools your parents used in your household. Parenting can be hard, especially when you've only ever peeked into the cockpit, but now you're supposed to fly the plane somehow. This is your moment to take both the issue and your own heart to God, asking him for clarity and truth.

Level-Two Conversations: Seeing Their Point of View

Think about when you were a teen. Yeah, back in the dark ages when phones were attached to the wall. The cigarettes passed around in your high school or puffed on in the parking lot may not be that different from today's vaping or juuling. When we began talking and writing about vaping, the research was inconclusive, but the research is catching up. More evidence is mounting about the harmful effects. Advertisers are marketing their products to a very young audience, and it's easy to move from flavored juices to nicotine to THC.

Vaping is often viewed by teens and tweens as a harmless, fun social activity, but there are a growing number of physical consequences resulting from vaping, including a possible link to cancer[2] and harmful effects on the heart and lungs.[3] Let's not forget that cigarettes were once viewed as harmless by our grandparents' generation. We have previous generations to study and prove the effects of cigarettes, but vaping is a new technology that has higher doses of new chemicals. Vaping is a big topic to understand, and more research will continue to develop after this book is in print.

Before you start this conversation or point to the research, put yourself in your children's shoes for a moment. It's helpful to weigh an issue like this without immediately reacting, which shuts down relationship. They need to see you trying to understand their perspective from the beginning. The old adage "Seek first to understand, then to be understood" is helpful for parents. Plus, making an effort not to approach them reactively, or out of fear or anger, will begin to put trust deposits in the bank. Sometimes it's easy to separate ourselves from the world-crushing problems of youth, but take just a moment and put yourself back in those years. Would you have been tempted to give vaping a try?

You can use this process we just walked through with any new situation. When you take time to slow down, breathe, and take this personal inventory, you will be more level-headed. Then you can respond honestly and compassionately from your own life experiences. When our brains are in a reactive state, honesty and compassion are hard to hang on to. When emotions are high, intelligence is low.

Exercise: Look back at a few of the "emergencies" you wrote down. Think back to when you were a teenager again. Name something similar you experienced. Why was it appealing? Why did you do it? Was there any resistance from your parents? Then, practice a calm reaction (the "I'm not shocked" face). Walk through the scenario in your head. Would you be angry, shocked, or sad if your teen answered these questions the way you did?

Now that you've taken a personal inventory and paused, you are ready to start talking with your teen. You've been doing the work. Up to this point we have only been working on you, your approach, your instincts, and your tone.

Some of you may be thinking, "My kid doesn't really do anything that I disagree with." They're not vaping, they don't drink, and they're not having sex. All of that's great, if it's true. However, you might be surprised what your kids could be hiding from you. Teens are master concealers, especially when they don't feel safe. A student once told us, "The stricter the parent, the sneakier the kid." Legalism is not a great alternative either. If we are not careful, churches, Christian schools, and ministries can breed legalistic rule followers with sour hearts or sneaky concealers.

This can be hard to think about, but let's zoom out and think about the long game here. Current stats say 60 to 70 percent of teens raised in a Christian environment will reject their faith when they leave for college. While your teen is under your roof, you get the chance to build a relationship with them, and we can't stress enough how crucial this is! You still have time.

Your teen doesn't have to be another fallout statistic. But we can't guarantee that extra conversations will help decide the future of your teen's faith. Some people hit a wall where they're left shaking their head, mumbling, "We did everything right, didn't we? But our kid went off the rails." If that's you, you're not alone. There is hope, and we want to be your guide through the messy and confusing parts of this beautiful opportunity called the teen years.

Level-Three Conversations: Lead with Curiosity

In level three, tone and posture are paramount. How amazing would it be if your teen walked away from a hard conversation thinking, "Mom just found out that I've been listening to Drake, vaping, or dating a boy secretly, and she didn't freak out. Maybe she actually cares about my world."

Curiosity is key to any relationship. This is why questions are so crucial on a first date. Curiosity shows caring and desire to know what's below the surface. It is important, however, to make sure your questions don't come across as accusatory. Developing an appreciation of your teen's culture, and even participating in it, is easier when you are curious instead of critical. A critical spirit kills conversation, but a curious heart cultivates discussion. Until you can first appreciate the culture they live in, your teen won't trust you to understand what they are experiencing. And until you can participate with them in their culture, they won't invite you into their story. Once they've invited you into their story, you'll begin to see their real struggles and the issues below their behaviors.

This may look like sitting down and letting them teach you how to play Fortnite or listening to their favorite song on the way to school. Eventually, your voice will become louder and louder, and outweigh the crowded voices. Being genuinely curious and asking questions in a way that is approachable and understanding lays the groundwork for a lifelong conversation. Remember, in the scheme of sixty years of conversation, you're just getting started!

The whole point of being curious is to connect with your teen and seek to understand the appeal. This allows you to discover the "why" behind the issue. Then you can take the conversations to the next level.

Exercise: Choose one of those new things your teen is participating in or consuming. If it is a cultural artifact, watch, listen, or consume it with your teen. Ask them some of these questions, developed by David Kinnaman of the Barna Group.

> "What did you find that is good in this song, movie, video game, etc.? Why do you believe it to be good?"
> "Is the artist saying anything about our world?"
> "Is there anything missing?"
> "What story is being told?"
> "Is there anything confusing?"
> "What does Scripture say about it?"

Level-Four Conversations: Continuation

Level four is where it all starts to come together. Here's what you've done so far.

- Assessment: You've assessed the situation and determined if it is worth addressing.
- Personal inventory: You've done a personal inventory of your background, how you would have responded as a teen, and have put yourself in their shoes.
- Curiosity: You've even started the conversation by asking questions with curiosity.

Now you're ready for level four: continuation. One way or another, your teen will respond to your questions. They may respond with poise and articulation, or they may respond with awkward mumbles. Whatever their response, the moment they look back at you to see your reaction, you're now at level four of the conversation.

They might shock you. They might irritate you. They might anger you. But your job is not to show any of it. Your "I'm not shocked" face is crucial if you want your teen to keep talking. Think of it as a parenting poker face with a twist. Engage. Smile. Listen. Show them you're for them no matter what. Breathe and bring your best "I'm not shocked" face. If you've had some outbursts with them in the past, this moment is especially valuable.

You are aiming to continue the conversation, not shut it down. From here you head back to level one, awareness of the topic. Assuming no emergencies come up, you're just taking a moment to pause, breathe, and consider the problem from their perspective (level two). Then you're asking another curious question to help you understand their world (level three). Remember, these are questions that don't incriminate, condemn, or shame. You're being curious to show them that you care.

This is the one-conversation model. It's a cycle. It repeats over the years with different micro conversations that lead to the conversation. It's a skill you will keep refining and choosing to engage with your teen. Fear, anger, and disengagement are easy, but meaningful engagement toward lifelong conversation takes intention. We hope you will experience this progression for many years to come.

Level one: Awareness—stop and evaluate if it's a real emergency.

Level two: Personal inventory—validate your own perspective and experience your teen's perspective.

Level three: Curiosity—ask warm, open-ended questions.

Level four: Continuation—keep the conversation going and repeat the cycle again and again with your teen.

After this point the levels might mesh together. The more you go through this, the faster it gets. Your teen will be responding, and you'll respond to them. Now you're literally in the flow of a dialogue. That's called a conversation.

Now you have a model for conversations. Stay aware of and continue walking through these four levels. Use this and practice it over and over again.

8

Two Types of Conversations

It was impossible to get a conversation going, everybody was talking too much.

Yogi Berra

While Jesus was having dinner at Levi's house, many tax collectors and sinners were eating with him and his disciples, for there were many who followed him.

Mark 2:15

Conversation isn't about proving a point; true conversation is about going on a journey with the people you are speaking with.

Ricky Maye

A family recently wrestled through a few tough situations. The couple had a ten-year-old son who was receiving love notes from a secret admirer. It was cute, and the suspense was building. After weeks of wondering who the secret admirer was, it turned out it was another boy. This was a shock to the family, and they needed to have some tricky conversations quickly. They downloaded one of our conversation kits, and they had some crucial conversations. Within a week a friend and neighbor messaged the son privately through a video game, sharing how he wanted to kill himself. Because the boy has a great relationship with his mom and dad, he shared this with them. They lifted the burden off his shoulders, helped him walk through another difficult situation, and were able to talk to the friend's parents and get that struggling child some help.

Culture is spinning faster than ever. Information is exploding and so is the rate of change. New technology, ideas, trends, words, topics, and dysfunctions are emerging, and our kids are wondering how to respond. This can create an ever-present sense of overwhelm. Youth culture is shaping all culture, but you feel more than a little in the dark. You're not immersed in the same hallways, apps, and conversations your teen is living in all day. It's normal for parents to feel this distance and to be overwhelmed. It can be hard to keep up.

Between your teen's sports practice, homework, time with friends, and the occasional good night's sleep, you don't have time to discuss every single thing in your teen's life. But don't let that discourage you from continuing this one lifelong conversation. As we continue discussing how to have these ongoing conversations with the teen you love, we want to help you clarify two kinds of conversations you need to be having regularly with your teen.

Now conversations: Other cultural conversations that are happening today or this week fall into the now category. They are new, and they are timely.

One aspect of now conversations are trends. Due to the evolution of the internet, social media, and smartphones in the lives of children and teens in the last decade, information and trends travel at light speed from pocket to pocket. This means there can be a worldwide phenomenon overnight. Remember Tide Pods, Momo, and the ice bucket challenge? By the time you read this you will be able to list dozens more from the past six months.

This is where it starts to get overwhelming. Not only do parents struggle to keep a base-level understanding of what their teens are doing and saying online, but speaking their language is extremely difficult, as it changes so fast. So, if you overhear your teen shout, "I just got merked," hopefully he's in the other room playing Fortnite and his character just died.

Another aspect of now conversations are topics. If a trend survives, it will become a common topic. These things are happening from one day to the next: emerging technologies, slang terms, artists, etc. For instance, Fortnite is still going strong at the release of this book. So is Snapchat.

Now conversations are important and need to be continually happening. But what about the always conversations? Take the theme of sexuality. There are tons of trends that have stuck around to create topics within sexuality. What is God's design for sex? Is it good, bad, or otherwise? How do you define gender? There's a bigger conversation around sexuality that answers these questions and continually needs to be addressed to be louder than the crowd of voices.

Always conversations: Some conversations will continually be happening. These are the big ones that span demographics, cultures, and generations. Your grandparents had them with your parents (or should have), and your parents had them with you. They are timeless.

Always conversations, by definition, are those big and daunting conversations. This is morality, truth, sexuality, purpose, justice, and even things such as economics. These are the types of conversations that you, as a caring adult, deeply desire to have with the teen you love. You want them to consider their faith and think through those 3,000 messages they're taking in every single day. Discussing themes with your teen is the deepest level of conversation. All these conversations are sacred, and some of them are scary. If the conversation seems scary (porn, gender, suicide, social media, drugs), you probably need to start it.

Sexuality is an always conversation. It might sound awkward, but you will always be talking about this with your teen in one way or another. How can you know all of the *now conversations* and the *always conversations*? It seems impossible.

Many parents assume that they shouldn't get too involved in their teen's lives. They fall to the disengaged side of the spectrum because they assume their teens don't want them "invading their space." They just stand on the periphery watching and hoping for good results. This sounds a lot like gambling. Others want to go big with every conversation, but their teens don't want them to go there. It's in their face, and a bit too much for their teen to handle. Walk these lines with discernment, but please keep walking them.

If you are a parent, we want you to learn to be a guide. There are two key actions that a parent takes to guide the conversation. We call them KNOW and GROW. KNOW means you spend a few minutes learning about a *topic* that you are *aware* of and that is impacting your teen *now*. You are taking the time to go a few steps deeper into their world. GROW means surrounding yourself with expert *teachers* who sharpen your skills on issues you are *unaware* of but that are *always* out there.

	NOW	ALWAYS
UNAWARE	Look *at* TRENDS	Grow *with* TEACHERS
AWARE	Know *the* TOPICS	Talk *about* THEMES

The Cloud of Voices

It can be hard to compete with social media, apps, smartphones, and the cornucopia of cultural offerings. Your teen is receiving messages every day through Netflix, ads in their music, sponsored content on Instagram, and old-school methods like billboards, flyers, and magazines. This is the cloud of voices. These things have power in your teen's life—and in your life too.

Let's not beat around the bush: Parenting teens is hard. And it only gets harder as your teen gets older. On top of that, there's an invisible clock counting down until they leave your home and your direct influence. It's inevitable for every parent. The closer your teen is to eighteen, the more crucial these real (yes, scary) conversations should be.

If you're feeling that tension, you're in the perfect place. You have the desire, the influence, and the wisdom to lead and teach your teen. Remember, the first half of the One Conversation model has you taking the time to focus on dealing with your problems, insecurities, and past before even having the conversation with your teen.

We believe God must be the main part of the equation for life-long faith. He will work through you and sometimes in spite of you in your teen's life. He is the only reason we have hope, and we've seen and heard stories that tell us it is possible for you and your teen to live a fulfilled life within the vision of the Gospel. Our goal at Axis is to better equip you to raise the kids God has entrusted to you in the midst of a culture that often goes against God's design.

We don't just want you to know the conversations you need to have, but we also want to arm you with a model for how to have these conversations. No, there aren't any shortcuts or parenting hacks, but all these tools will make it a little easier to cut through the cultural clutter. We've discussed the four levels of the conversation. Do you remember the progression of conversation we shared in the previous chapter?

Level one: Awareness—stop and evaluate if it's a real
emergency.

Level two: Personal inventory—validate your own perspective
and experience your teen's perspective.

Level three: Curiosity—ask warm, open-ended questions.

Level four: Continuation—keep the conversation going and
repeat the cycle again and again with your teen.

Remember all the work you've done up to this point. Many
parents want to jump straight to theme-style conversations, and
sometimes fall into the trap of dictating the morality, truth, or
sexuality instead of discussing the large, nuanced themes. Doing
this is understandable, but it's just not effective. It's nearly impossible to effect change on the theme level with your teen if you
haven't already covered the trends and topics.

With the One Conversation model, there are steps you must walk
through first. You've showed interest in your teen's world, you've
done a personal inventory, and you've asked questions. Rinse and
repeat for years to come.

Let's walk through an example of what this could look like
in your life. Let's focus on Fortnite. It's one of the most popular
video games. It's stirring up a lot of fear in parents, because it's a
first-person shooter game in the age of school shootings.

Look below the what to the why. Why is your teen spending
hours on this? What's the appeal? Perhaps they are discouraged
and lacking confidence. Maybe they feel like they can win in Fortnite and can't really win anywhere else. Or all their closest friends
play, and they don't want to be left out. Maybe it's just fun.

Don't forget this: You and your teen are not the only two parties
involved in this equation. God is active here. God is in the midst
of all these questions in this conversation.

We like the way *The Message* paraphrases John 15:4–5: "Live
in me. Make your home in me just as I do in you. In the same way

that a branch can't bear grapes by itself but only by being joined to the vine, you can't bear fruit unless you are joined with me. I am the Vine, you are the branches. When you're joined with me and I with you, the relation intimate and organic, the harvest is sure to be abundant. Separated, you can't produce a thing."

God may be doing something below the surface you're not aware of. We recommend constantly having these questions in the back of your mind as you cycle through these four levels of conversation: *What's good? What's bad? What's missing? What's confused? And what do the Scriptures say?*

You're still the parent or caring adult. You have not surrendered your authority, but you need to express some curiosity instead of just rebuke. You've entered into a more nuanced conversation than a level-one parent. It's the tension of the messy middle, the third way, but it's right where you need to be.

It's incredibly honoring to your teen to live at level four instead of level one. There is dignity here. There is respect for the reality that they are stretching and growing into an adult. The more you use this model, the more you'll become aware of the trends, topics, teachers, and themes influencing your teen every day. Show curiosity and they'll actually start to teach you. Eventually, fewer emergencies will arise, because the big problems that come down the line will be ones you've already dealt with bit by bit, and as they come they will be less intense and overwhelming. Then, it'll become easier to live in the theme level of conversation. The theme level is the deepest, but remember: As you walk through all four levels, whether it's about the latest video game or a troubling cultural trend, every conversation builds trust with your teen.

We know this is a lot to process. As we approach larger cultural themes, parent fear can spike. You don't suddenly turn into an expert on emerging culture or teen trends. Our team continues to dig for the latest trends and translate culture so you can have these conversations with your teen. We spend all week creating resources on the latest emerging topics that balance changing culture with the unchanging Gospel of Jesus.

We don't know everything, but we are passionate about equipping you to have one conversation with the teen you love. We want to arm you with what you need to start, kick-start, and restart your ongoing conversation with your kid every single day for the rest of your lives. New things will emerge for *now conversations*, but you'll still be having the *always conversations*, too. Don't let fear scare you away from conversation.

TOPICS YOU NEED TO ENGAGE WITH YOUR TEEN

9

The New Sex Talk

The problem is not that pornography shows too much of the person, but that it shows far too little.

Pope John Paul II

Above all else, guard your heart, for everything you do flows from it.

Proverbs 4:23

When one is loved, she can create better.

Ana Roš, world-famous chef

A popular girl at school was getting a lot of attention from the boys. One guy continued to ask her for a nude photo. Finally, he wore her down by asking her repeatedly, and she sent it. He then shared it with a lot of other boys at the school. They mocked her and shamed her, calling her "slut" and "ho." Another group of girls who were not getting the same attention from guys looked on enviously. One of those girls commented, "I wish boys would ask me for nude photos."

This has become a common phenomenon. Girls have started sending nude photos to guys to get their attention. One boy was the talk of so many girls at school that they started sending him nudes to get his attention. So many girls in the school sent him nude photos that he saw a business opportunity and sold those photos. Another boy used violent threats to procure photos, saying he would kill a certain girl if she didn't send him a nude photo within six days. As the girl's fear grew and day six approached, she sent it to him, and he sold the photos to other boys.

Sisters at a Christian school were badgered for nude photos. Their predator wasn't an older man in a sting operation on TV— he was a teenage boy.

These stories are perverted and terrifying. Sex has become twisted and instantly accessible. The tools at our teens' disposal are extremely powerful. Teen expert Mark Gregston writes, "I'm never surprised when a young lady sends nude pictures of herself to guys just to get someone to pay attention to her. It's the cathedral apex of a desire to be noticed, coupled with a teen's world of shallow relationships, where every teen carries a camera. It's a scream communicating, 'Look at me! Will someone just pay attention to me?'"[1]

Those stories are enough to make any parent want to throw their kid's smartphone off a bridge. But third-way parents choose to see the dangers, breathe deep, ask God for wisdom, and lean into the messy middle. While it's tempting to villainize everything around technology, hold on a minute. Keep reading.

Kids wield powerful tools, but don't naturally have the discernment to handle them. "The world convinces teens they are capable of much more than they actually are," writes Gregston.[2] This means they believe that things won't be a problem for them, and that they can handle it. Beyond practices such as sexting, views of sexuality are loosening at an incredible rate. Kids are being exposed to thinking that is drastically different from the notions of sexuality their parents and grandparents grew up with.

Here's what Miley Cyrus says about her sexuality:

> I am literally open to every single thing that is consenting and doesn't involve an animal, and everyone is of age.[3]

Here's Lily-Rose Depp's (Johnny Depp's daughter) view:

> You don't have to label your sexuality; so many kids these days are not labeling their sexuality, and I think that's so cool. . . . If you like something one day, then you do, and if you like something else the other day, it's whatever. You don't have to label yourself because it's not set in stone. It's so fluid.[4]

Think about the sexual vernacular kids are growing up with today. Lesbian, gay, bisexual, transgender, transsexual, queer, questioning, intersex, asexual, ally, pansexual. That is a lot to process, and it's confusing to teens. Yeah, we know, it's confusing to adults too! Human beings are amazingly complex. We are motivated by desires for significance, success, meaning, love, intimacy—but all porn shows of a person is their physical sexuality. And a false airbrushed sexuality at that.

But before we go any further, we need to say this: Sex is a very good thing. The desire for sex is a gift from God. And when expressed in its proper context, within marriage between a man and woman, it is one of the greatest gifts that God gives us. That needs to frame the conversation as we push into sexual misuses.

However, sex can become a quick way to be seen. Pediatrician Meg Meeker says, "While it's easy to lose hope as we look at behavior trends such as teenage drinking, drug and sex rates we see great potential on the other side of this. Amidst the boundary pushing and arguments, below it all your daughter is actually asking, 'Am I worth the fight, Dad?'"[5] This is one reason we are big fans of dads giving devoted time and attention to their daughter!

She needs to know that she lights you up and that you love her for who she is, not what she looks like.

After conversations with countless teen girls around sexuality, here is what Dr. Meeker has concluded:

> Parent connectedness is the number-one factor in preventing girls from engaging in premarital sex and indulging in drugs and alcohol.[6]
>
> 97% of girls who said they could talk to their parents had lower teen pregnancy rates.[7]

These stats reveal a deeper story. Parents, your daughter wants your attention. Your fear for your daughter is real. It means you love her. She wants to be seen and known. Show her you love her with your presence, your words, and your attention, not your fear.

However warped and twisted our desires may have become, all of them, including sexual desire, have their original root in God's good design. But we're faced with a paradox because even good desires bring the potential for pain—specifically, the pain that comes when we don't get what we want.

Sex is as casual and easy as ever. Apps are designed specifically to help you get it easily. In their book *Good Faith*, David Kinnaman and Gabe Lyons state, "Sex is ubiquitous and easily accessible— and now marriage is no longer the barrier to entry that it once was." The low price of sex can be seen in the increasing brokenness and low esteem of marriage. "Among the goals twentysomethings want to achieve before they turn thirty, marriage doesn't crack the top five."[8] These shifts around marriage are impacting shifts around sexuality. There are many different reactions to the role of sexual desire and the pain it often causes.

On one end of the spectrum is the stoic mindset that some interpretations of Buddhism promote. This says that the way to eliminate that pain and suffering is to eliminate all desire. If you don't desire something, you'll never feel pain from not having it.

But of course, if we desire not to have desires . . . we're still stuck in desire. As caring adults, it's easy to fall into this as we tell teens, "Don't do that, care about that, or want that!" It's really not that easy.

On the other end of the spectrum is the message to embrace your desires above all else. A barrage of messaging tells us, "Do whatever feels good now!" "Run after your heart," and "You do you!" Of course, this feels right momentarily and leaves a wake of consequences behind us.

Songs, shows, and movies are whispering to live for today—that it's all that matters anyway. Part of the challenge for helping teens grow in wisdom is teaching (and modeling) delayed gratification in an instant culture. And sex is one of the hardest areas in which to communicate this.

Solomon, David, and Samson on Sex

Three of our biblical heroes fell prey to the trap of misplaced sex: Solomon, David, and Samson. Solomon, the wisest and richest man in the Bible, had all that he should have needed to be satisfied. But he could not overcome the temptation to leverage his power to take hundreds of wives and corrupt the kingdom. David, the man after God's own heart, the man with incredible purpose and connection with God, gave in to sexual sin and had an affair with Bathsheba. Samson, "the strong man of Scripture," with arguably the most raw power of anyone in the Bible, gave in to sexual temptation with his inappropriate relationship with Delilah.

We would have to be richer than Solomon, closer to God than David, and stronger than Samson if we hoped to defeat sexual sin on our own. If you feel unworthy of discussing sex with your teen because of your own sexual past, don't let that defeat you. There is restoration and healing for you. Without Jesus, we are all hopeless. The good news is Jesus' sacrifice and resurrection defeated the power of sin and in him we have hope. You are a new creation. You aren't who you used to be, and you can share that with your teen as a powerful example of God transforming a life.

Remember, no matter how inadequate you feel, the same power that raised Christ from the dead is at work in us, helping us to say no to temptation and sin and yes to holiness. The words of 1 Corinthians 10:13 can bring a sense of comfort: "No temptation has overtaken you except what is common to mankind. And God is faithful; he will not let you be tempted beyond what you can bear. But when you are tempted, he will also provide a way out so that you can endure it."

You can walk alongside your teen in their struggles, even sexual ones, instead of having them feel alone in them. Encourage your teen to plan wisely ahead of time to avoid tempting situations, but also look for the way out when they are tempted with their phone, computer, or in the back seat of a car. In the moments when we are tempted, we have to partner with God to find that way out.

But Christ not only frees us from our sin, he also fulfills our desires for satisfaction, purpose, and freedom.

We love this definition of parenting from Mark Gregston: "The role parents (and grandparents) have in today's culture is to maintain a household of love, preserving the rules and boundaries that help keep a child on the right path, while encouraging independence and responsibility."[9] You can, indeed, hold boundaries and encourage independence at the same time. That's the tension third-way parents walk in.

Fences

One of the greatest roles and challenges of parents is teaching wisdom. "The beginning of wisdom is this: Get wisdom. Though it cost all you have, get understanding" (Proverbs 4:7).

For many of you, especially with firstborns, it's tempting to sling fear instead of teaching wisdom. It's easier to just say, "Don't do the bad stuff! Come on!" But third-way parents must be in the business of teaching wisdom. It requires thinking in two ways.

Fence off the bad: We would never play soccer by a cliff without a fence. That game ends poorly. Part of parenting is putting down boundaries to protect from the terrible stuff, the pain our kids could easily inflict on themselves.

Fence in the good: But soccer next to a cliff can be fun—if there is a fence. It allows the fun without fear of freefall. The stress and anxiety are gone so we can freely play the game.

If you want to walk the journey of a third-way parent, you'll need to fence off the bad and fence in the good. Boundaries create safety and develop wisdom. Safety creates both freedom and trust. The family must be a place of safety so children can grow into healthy adults. "All the really important things we do as families involve developing wisdom," writes Andy Crouch.[10] Eventually your kids will have to learn to build their own fences. They'll have to learn to self-govern in every aspect of life. They'll have to learn to drive their own car, manage their own time, put limits on their smartphone, and create more than they consume.

So while we put limits on screen time, the App Store, and what time they come home, it's okay for them to know they can't handle freedom without limits yet. They need to grow into it. You don't trust their searches and downloads yet, and you want to help protect their future marriage, family, and fulfillment. They can't choose moderation yet, but someday they will. Boundaries are always a long-term play. And they're not going to thank you for these boundaries for years to come.

Fences are built through intentional conversations and the setting of boundaries. Remember, your teen will feel initially that fences are limiting them. Make sure to talk about the beauty of sex in the right space, the pleasure and fulfillment it brings inside marriage. But talk about how counterfeit sex (porn, hookup apps, sexting, and casual partners) erode the intention of good sex. Porn is ripping through marriages, creating distrust and divorce, which only compounds societal problems. There is also research on how porn desensitizes the mind to sex, leading to impotence earlier in life (which no teenage boy will believe). While it may feel awkward to have these conversations, if you don't have the timeless and timely conversations with your kids, the cloud of voices on Google, YouTube, and apps will.

On some level, we all still experience longings and desires that cannot be fulfilled in this life. The total fulfillment of our desires will be experienced one day when we have perfect relationship with God. Point your teen toward the eternal and ask God to give them a vision for their future.

Isaiah talks about the joy we will experience on that day.

> Those the Lord has rescued will return.
> They will enter Zion with singing;
> everlasting joy will crown their heads.
> Gladness and joy will overtake them,
> and sorrow and sighing will flee away.
>
> Isaiah 51:11

We long for heaven's banquet table, but we eat appetizers now. We try unsuccessfully to make good things, sex included, the fullness of what God has for us. When we dwell in eternity with Christ, we will never want or need again. We will be fully satisfied, purposeful, and free in him. No shame. No perversion. No one asking for nude photos.

Obviously, this chapter does not cover the full gamut of sexuality and everything you should discuss with your teen. We have parent guides and conversation kits on the specifics.

10

Smartphones

Technology is only very good if it can help us become the persons we were meant to be.

Andy Crouch[1]

Rules without relationship may cause rebellion. Relationships without rules cause chaos.

Mark Gregston[2]

The more I considered Christianity, the more I found that while it had established a rule and order, the chief aim of that order was to give room for good things to run wild.

G. K. Chesterton, *Orthodoxy*

A mom noticed her middle school-aged son looking a bit off. When she approached him, he said people online were sending him awful videos, first of kittens being killed, then a first-person shooter video. He was visibly disturbed. This had such an impact on his heart and mind that he helped her set up technology filters so his younger siblings wouldn't be exposed to things like that.

Technology is a conundrum for parents and kids. Parents have the wisdom of the dangers, but don't know how to set up the technology around it. Kids know how to set up the technology, but don't have the wisdom of the dangers. That's why we need copious conversations and a close relationship so we can work together on this. One parent shared with our Axis team, "Having a teenager is like having live-in tech support."

Thanks to the famous 2007 announcement of an innovative new phone, the iPhone, nearly everything has changed. Smartphones are the number-one thing parents reach out to us about. Not only have we dedicated a chapter to them, we wrote a whole book about how to manage them called *Smartphone Sanity*. The smartphone is shaping our culture, and it's shaping our teens. Here is our perspective.

> The smartphone is the new university.
> The smartphone is the new parent.
> The smartphone is the modern Swiss Army knife.
> The smartphone will disciple your teen if you don't.

This glorious and problematic smartphone has become the rectangular modern-day Swiss Army knife. What can't it do?! This supercomputer is in the pockets of preteens and teens everywhere. The smartphone is the engine accelerating the shifts in teen culture. As one dad put it, "I always feel three apps behind my kids." And we know from interacting with thousands of parents that the smartphone is the number-one battleground over which parents and teens fight. The times, they are a-changin', and this can be overwhelming. It will make even the best of us want to retreat into our time machines and head back to the "good old days" (which weren't that good, by the way).

But let us assure you all is not lost. Actually, there are incredible opportunities for you to invest in your children and help rewire the way they interact with technology and the messages it transfers. No, it doesn't involve throwing all screens off a cliff or giving open access to them. The opportunity lies in reframing the conversation through "smartphone discipleship." This can affirm a deeper way of being human as you connect your wisdom with your teen's wonder.

Here are four conversations to have with the teen you love about technology, specifically the smartphone.

Conversation One: Very Good, Cursed, and Redeemed

Dr. Sherry Turkle, director of the MIT Initiative on Technology and Self, once said, "Computers are not good or bad; they are powerful."[3] Turkle's statement is just as provocative in a day when most teenagers use their smartphones as their primary computers. We agreed with this statement for over a year (whoops!), but then one day we stopped and started to rethink it. Does the Bible really say that the world God made, including the technology created from it, is not "good or bad" but neutral? Actually, in Genesis it says the exact opposite: God weaves the world together and then declares that it is "very good."

Part of that goodness includes the command God gave man and woman to cultivate the earth. In essence, we are living out the image of God imprinted on us when we create. In our view, technology— like any tool we've created—is simply one way humans have cultivated the "very good" cosmos. But the story doesn't end there. This very good world has been subjected to the curse since Adam and Eve chose to rebel against God. Thus, cultivation—and therefore all technology—is affected by that curse. So rather than being neutral, technology is both very good and cursed. And of course, the story doesn't end there either. God is committed to his creation, and through the death, burial, and resurrection (and way, truth, and life) of Jesus, God is redeeming that creation. The best part is that we are invited into that mission with him. Think about that for a second. We are joining God again, this time in redeeming what has been lost. So here's the first important conversation to have with your teen: *How is a smartphone (or anything) very good, how is it cursed, and how can we as a family redeem it?*

This positioning is huge. You are no longer the bad guy, and you are no longer making the cool new piece of technology evil. Instead, you are inviting that technology into a bigger story, into the story of God. And while doing that, you are humbly submitting that form of technology to the rule of God.

Conversation Two: What Is It For?

When it comes to technology, we will quickly confess: We like it. It's fun, interesting, and powerful. Of course, it can be massively distracting and, in some cases, flat-out dangerous. The second conversation to have about any form of technology is this: *What is it for?* Although it seems like a deceptively simple question, how you and your children answer the question of purpose ultimately determines how you ought to use that technology. So what is a smartphone for? Maybe your family would say that it's connecting us with the ones we love the most. Okay, great!

Now fast-forward to dinnertime. Your family is at a restaurant, and dad is checking email, mom is on Pinterest, and daughter is keeping her Snapstreak going. Whoops!

How about Netflix? What is it for? Sure, it's an incredible library of long-form TV shows with a few movies thrown in. What a fun way to learn and be entertained by great storytelling. But the Oompa Loompas see TV differently:

> IT ROTS THE SENSE IN THE HEAD!
> IT KILLS IMAGINATION DEAD!
> IT CLOGS AND CLUTTERS UP THE MIND!
> IT MAKES A CHILD SO DULL AND BLIND!

HE CAN NO LONGER UNDERSTAND
A FANTASY, A FAIRYLAND!
HIS BRAIN BECOMES AS SOFT AS CHEESE!
HIS POWERS OF THINKING RUST AND FREEZE!
HE CANNOT THINK—HE ONLY SEES![4]

Understanding the intended purpose and subsequently the actual outcome needs to be an ongoing conversation. If the diet we're on is causing us to be unhealthy, we should correct our course. If the smartphone that's supposed to connect us really just pulls us apart, it's time to go back to the drawing board.

Conversation Three: We Are on a Journey with a Destination

When I (David) was in high school, I was eager to turn sixteen so I could drive. To my advantage, my parents were equally eager to stop being my personal Uber. As a family we began the process of getting my driver's license. Getting a license can be a pretty intimidating process. You need to take a course, then pass a test (that most people fail the first time), then you apply to receive your permit. In some states, you need to have your permit for a year before you can get your license. And while you have your permit, you take lessons from a professional driving instructor and log hours while driving supervised, both during the day and at night. Finally, you take a driving test with your state's department of motor vehicles. Oh, and while doing this, you might be purchasing a vehicle, applying for insurance, and trying to learn your way around town.

We think you should take a similar mindset with smartphones. In the same way you don't hand your kids the keys with no training and say, "Good luck," you shouldn't hand them a smartphone and say, "What could go wrong?" Their lives, your life, and others' lives hang in the balance physically, legally, and spiritually. In short, we advise against giving your children a phone if you are not ready to have a conversation with them about it multiple times a week for multiple years.

Also, when you're teaching them how to drive, the goal is for them to drive on their own without you in the passenger seat forever. The same is true for smartphones: You don't want to be skimming all their texts for the rest of your life. Ain't nobody got time for that! Which brings us to the third conversation in smartphone discipleship. Your family is on a journey together of enjoying, leveraging, and self-regulating your phones. And there is a destination. You have arrived when your children have demonstrated integrity and have learned how to self-regulate their phones and no longer have limits imposed by you; they impose their own limits. Usually this happens in their junior or senior year of high school.

Milestones on the "Smartphone Ed" Journey

Goal: Focus on their heart with a view on righteousness.

Practice: Start with the end in mind.

Always start with your teen's heart in mind and zoom out with the end of the journey in sight. Your goal is to mentor your child so that his or her heart loves righteousness. This goes so much deeper than behavior management. You want your child to be able to use a phone with wisdom and joy, and without your oversight. You want your teenager to be independent and able to self-regulate.

Goal: Journey toward ownership.

Practice: Stewardship through leasing.

If God owns everything, He owns all phones. As a parent, you are responsible to God as the ultimate steward of your child's phone. A great way to help steward your children's hearts and phones is by making a family contract that they sign in order to "lease" their phones from you. There are many great contracts online that you can use for inspiration. Also, consider having your child contribute financially to the costs involved with the phone.

Goal: Easing into privacy.
Practice: Accountability in community.

We are better in community than in isolation. We recommend that you have access to the phone at any time and have access to all login information and settings. This sounds harsh, but your child does not have a right to phone privacy. Explain that privacy is earned through demonstrating integrity, and that even adults often relinquish this right to others in order to steer clear of temptation or misuse of their phones. Make sure you are modeling community to your kids.

If things escalate and you must take your teen's phone away, always remember that to the next generation, a phone is an extension of their identity. Ironically, teens run to others through their phone for comfort. Teens who once simply had to choose their parents as their source of comfort when they were stressed, anxious, or sad can now turn to acquaintances or "friends" all over the world to comfort them or spray random advice at them.[5] When you take their phone away, you are literally taking away part of who they are and their access to community. Never take it away lightly, and when you do, clearly explain what needs to happen before you to give it back.

Goal: Giving incremental responsibility.
Practice: Increase freedom slowly.

Phones are amazing and can accomplish thousands of functions. Upon first leasing your children a phone, we recommend you severely limit the phone's functionality. Be warned, this may be a point of contention, but it's a great opportunity to refer to the contract you had them sign. Remind them that as they learn to wisely use their phones, over time they will have fewer and fewer restrictions. There are great time-limiting apps for Apple, iOS, and Android devices (Screen Time and Google Family Line, for example) and filters you can add around almost anything. Many of these tools are great for limiting your own screen time too.

What We Recommend When They First Get a Phone

The App Store should never be left on and should be restricted. Any app on the phone should require your approval to download and update. You should know what each app is for, in-app purchases should be turned off, and apps should not be allowed to be deleted without permission. Also, check all apps, especially ones buried multiple folders deep. Over time, you will want to and should give them the keys to the App Store, but don't let them delete apps.

Texting/email should not be allowed unless you have access to all messages on a mirrored and separate device. Here's the principle behind this: seeing themselves being seen. Eventually, you'll get bored and can stop skimming their messages because you trust them. Trust the Holy Spirit to prompt you to check your kids' messages when something is awry.

Social media is not allowed until trust and open communication are proven. Our reasoning is that there's really no way to monitor social media. If you do at some point choose to allow your child to have a social media account, proceed with caution and be aware of the mental and emotional health problems that can be caused or triggered by social media. We highly recommend that parents join whatever social media platform their kids are on. It's beneficial for you to experience it and have the credibility to host the "What is it for?" conversation.

Keep in mind that if you have given them your trust regarding social media, asking them before you "follow" them will reiterate your faith in them. Also take some time to study and learn social media etiquette and dos and don'ts. We'd hate for you to "heart" your own Instagram post.

Internet browsers need to be filtered and have built-in accountability reporting. There are obvious sexual risks involved with full access to the internet, not to mention sexual predators. Think of a filter like a wall. A wall helps, but if you're clever, you can always find a way around it. Your long-term goal should be to help your kids understand what triggers them so they can willingly build their own wall. The best wall is not actually a filter, but a community of friends and mentors to whom they are accountable. And by the way, none of this will work if you are not first modeling it.

Boundaries for All of You

We asked a thirteen-year-old what her plans were for the evening. She responded, "I'm going to go home and watch my parents stare at their phones." Steve Jobs purposely designed Apple devices without an off switch. Sometimes the only way to be fully present is to shut our phones off. Here are some things we've seen great families do to limit the incessant beckoning of their phones.

Limit apps and notifications. Some parents refuse to have email on their phones because it causes them to work at home instead of enjoying their families. Some parents turn off notifications for social media and even texting because they know they check them enough already.

Agree to a technology curfew for all devices in the evening and the morning. A helpful curfew is no devices from 8 p.m. to 8 a.m. We recommend setting a gentle alarm that goes off at 8 p.m. every night to remind you of the curfew. Make it the bad guy. Too many humans are sleeping directly next to devices, and it's messing with our sleep. Seventy percent of parents sleep with their device next to them, as do 72 percent of preteens, and 82 percent of teens.[6]

Limit or forbid devices in the bedroom, especially at night. Buy everyone alarm clocks and charge all of their devices in a common area while everyone sleeps. This helps the devices stay charged during the day, helps everyone sleep better at night, and helps the family avoid temptations.

Decide on time limits for devices, and then keep track. This very good device can become cursed pretty quickly when it distracts us from creating and only encourages us to mindlessly consume. Without limits, the good stuff of life as a family can zoom past us while our heads are down.

When we speak to parents, we ask, "When you parent, what is your greatest competition?" You may be surprised by the answer. A parent's greatest competition is . . . other parents. Here's what we mean. Just as your teen experiences peer pressure, you will experience pressure from other parents regarding smartphones and discipleship. You're going to have to call some tough shots and graciously disagree with how other parents set boundaries for their own kids. Know that this is normal, and don't be discouraged. Always stay humble, be teachable, and stick to your convictions. Remember to have this conversation: We are on a journey with a destination.

Conversation Four: You Can Tell Me Anything

I (David) had just finished a rather energetic discussion with a teen about tech limits her parents had placed on her phone when she quipped, "The stricter the parent, the sneakier the child." What a zinger! At first her statement feels true, then it feels false, then you eventually realize there are some hidden assumptions behind her declaration. This teen was assuming her parents didn't have her best interest at heart and, ultimately, that God didn't have her best interest at heart.

Do you want your teen to run to you or away from you? Instead of pointing our index fingers at our teens and saying, "You're being sneaky," we need to ask deeper questions.

"Do you believe I am 'for' you?"

"Do you believe God's path is good?"

"Do you believe it leads to life, flourishing, joy, and meaning?"

When your kids say, "You are being too strict!" it might be good to reflect: *Do my kids know I have their best interests at heart? Am I safe, quick to forgive, and eager to reconcile?* And here's the real mind grenade to reflect upon: Are you raising a sin concealer or a sin confessor?[7] The only way to know the answer to this question is to ask yourself, *Do I model confession and forgiveness to my children?*

The "I'm Not Shocked" Face

You want your kids to be able to tell you anything, right? You need to convince them they can trust you enough to be honest with you. There will be some awkward conversations you'll wish you could avoid, but if they don't hear the truth from you, who's going to tell them? A couple of genius parents introduced us to the "I'm not shocked" face. Whenever you hear something shocking from your child and your insides are turning, or you need to talk with them about something tough, you can't show it. Your calm exterior invites trust, and your freaked-our exterior convinces them they can't share things like that.

Ready to practice your "I'm not shocked" face? Here are some awkward topics you need to consistently bring up with your smartphone-wielding preteens and teens.

Pornography. We hate to say this, but your children will more than likely see porn. The average age of exposure keeps getting younger. They need to know that they can talk with you about this. They need to know what to do when they come across it. They also need you to help them define a beautiful and realistic view of sexuality.

Sexting. Reread the last chapter. Sexting has become a normal part of dating. If you have a daughter, there's a good chance she will be solicited for nude pictures. Many girls who are not asked for nudes want boys to ask them. Are you practicing your "I'm not shocked" face?! Remember, they want to be wanted, and this is how culture is telling them to measure their value. Encourage your children never to send suggestive pictures of themselves, never to pass along suggestive images, and to tell you immediately when they receive them. Let them know that they can blame you in order to scare their friends into not sending them nudes.

Sneaky apps. There are some apps that are designed specifically to deceive parents. Notoriously, a calculator app that looks like a calculator and works like a calculator, but entering a secret numerical password reveals a hidden folder in which children can hide pictures from their parents.

Fake social media accounts. Don't be surprised if your son or daughter has multiple accounts on the same social media platform. One is for parents (and grandma, too!), and the other is a place to have unmonitored conversations with friends. Ask your children if they have a Finstagram (i.e., a fake Instagram).

Friends' phones. Finally, you've had enough of (fill in the blank) app. Your son has crossed the line too many times, so you're going to take his phone away for a long, long time. Or maybe you're frustrated that your time machine won't take you back to the 1950s, so you vow never to let your kid have a smartphone. There's one small problem: Your teen can still borrow a friend's phone. On a friend's phone, your child can manage social media and have access to porn, sexts, and all the depths of the internet.

Sure, you can go to Goodwill and buy a rotary phone and a VCR, but we encourage the third way, where you courageously pursue your child's heart. Frequently remind them of your unshakable love and that you've got their back. Since day one you've had their best interests at heart, and no matter what they're up against, they can come to you for a listening ear, support, and even to confess their mistakes.

Snapchat Missionary

Remember, you're a missionary to your kid. By the grace of God and the guidance of the Holy Spirit, seek to reach into their world, just like Jesus did for all of humanity. This may mean limiting your freedom for a season to join them in a technology fast, or it may mean giving up your phone privacy to lead by example and show that you have nothing to hide. It could also mean downloading Snapchat (or whatever their go-to app is) simply to understand what they love about it. We encourage you to spend thirty minutes a week studying your teens' world so you can better connect with them.

Being a missionary begins with curiosity. Seek to understand their reality: Bullying not only happens in person, but also online 24/7, male/female orientation isn't a given, identity feels dependent on "likes," and sexting is an expected part of dating. You have what it takes, and we believe in you! Hold fast to your heart connection with your child and hold fast to continuing the one conversation.

11

Video Games[1]

If Pac-Man had affected us as kids, we'd all be running around in dark rooms, munching pills and listening to repetitive electronic music.

British comedian and actor, Marcus Brigstocke[2]

Technology is creating a busyness and ongoing distraction that is getting in the way of real spiritual conversations.

The Barna Group[3]

A game is an opportunity to focus our energy, with relentless optimism, at something we're good at (or getting better at) and enjoy. In other words, gameplay is the direct emotional opposite of depression.

Jane McGonigal, *Reality Is Broken*

You walk in the door with your arms full of groceries only to find your son in the exact position playing the exact same video game as when you left. His eyes are glazed over, and he doesn't even acknowledge you. You've been trying to enforce boundaries and limits on his video gaming, but it only ends in tension and conflict.

You're not alone. Few topics in today's media-saturated world can get parents so frustrated and confused.

Parents have many questions about video games, which have changed infinitely since we were kids. They're better than the pixilated Atari and Nintendo 64 games we used to play. Video games have had a bad reputation with child psychologists since the '80s, when home gaming first became affordable for the average family. Technology has improved vastly, and gaming has exploded. The effects, music, voiceovers, graphics, and objectives are insane.

In this chapter we want to give you information about video games, but also offer processes to connect to the heart of your teen. While the games are easy to villainize, we want you to take steps toward engaging with your kids on them and developing wisdom through them. One dad we know agreed to buy his kids a Wii and play it with them as long as they also played the real games. So, they'd play Wii bowling one night, and then follow that with a trip to the bowling alley. Eventually, his kids decided the real thing was far better than the video-game version, and their family carved out special times to play games together. Well done, dad!

Games are a challenge and an escape. They offer entertainment and rewards that social media platforms don't. Teens say they enjoy gaming as a way to "blow off steam" from the stress of the day—homework, friend dynamics, family pressures, bullying, chores, picking colleges, choosing career paths, getting jobs, and the general weirdness of navigating the teen years.

More important, teens love video games for their narrative element. Today's games are fully immersive experiences that invite players into a dynamic and complex story line in which they play a part. This will only increase with virtual reality (VR) becoming more affordable. Unlike movies or books that allow you to experience a story from the outside, video games give you the control over a character and their actions. They are an immersion into a new story. Cutting-edge visuals and audio draw us into a new reality. Teens aren't just watching a new story unfold, they are participating in it.

Innovations in game design and platforms now allow teens to socialize while gaming—they invite friends to play, chat, text, make new friends, work together to form teams and strategies, and satiate their competitive drive. With the explosion of E-sports, some can even turn what was once considered a mind-numbing time waster with no real benefit into a career.

Despite all the stereotypes, males aren't the only ones playing video games. A 2018 Pew Research study found that 97 percent of teen boys and 83 percent of teen girls said they play video games in some form or fashion. The increase in both male and female players could be due to a number of reasons (more mobile games, higher smartphone ownership among teens, higher gaming console ownership, more collaborative games, different types of games, the success of Fortnite, etc.), but it's clear that this is no longer just a male pastime. Oh yeah, and don't be surprised to find your kid intently watching someone else play a video game online.

Gamers are no longer basement-dwelling loners. With today's communication technology embedded in their games, they are free to develop friendship dynamics with online players, as they do with in-person play. Gaming can improve cognitive skills, problem-solving, decision making, strategic thinking, attention level, manual dexterity, computer literacy, and can help kids in reading, math, and science. It increases teens' interest in STEM topics and improves their ability to process visual information quickly and correctly. Many games even take place in historically accurate times and places, piquing the interest of teens who ordinarily would roll their eyes at the sight of a history text. Schools are using video games for learning development as early as kindergarten.

Let's Talk about Ratings

Video game ratings are created by the nonprofit Entertainment Software Rating Board. They help to ensure responsible web and mobile privacy practices. Their ratings have three components:

Rating Categories, which suggest age appropriateness.

Content Descriptors, which indicate content that may have triggered a specific rating and may possibly be of interest or concern.

Interactive Elements, which highlight interactive or online features of a product, including users' ability to interact with each other, the sharing of users' locations with other users, if purchases of digital goods or services are offered, or if unrestricted internet access is provided.

The ratings are designated as follows:

E: Everyone

E10+: Everyone 10 years old and above

T: Teen

M: Mature (17+)

A: Adults only (18+)

It's important to note that they only call the ratings *guidance* for parents, meaning that they've created a system for *everyone* that inherently can't work perfectly for *individual* families and gamers. It's important to use the ratings as a baseline, then do some research on a game before deciding whether a specific child should play it or not. You're still the parent.

The Struggles around Video Games

Limits. Parents have a hard time enforcing boundaries on video-game play with their kids. Teens can play practically anywhere: on home-based consoles, personal computers, smartphones, tablets, handheld consoles, social media, school computers, at a friend's home, and at stores that sell games. The internet has no shortage of free games available to users—games of all types with no regulation of content or age limitations for players. It's impossible to have complete control over their length of gaming time and the types of games they access. Additionally, their friends' parents may not adhere to the content or time limits you set for your kids, and they could also differ widely on morality and judging appropriate gaming content for kids.

Violence. Perhaps the best-known debate about video games is the potential harm of violence portrayed in-game. According to the American Psychological Association, 85 percent of video games contain some form of violence.[4] In 2011, the US Supreme Court rejected a ban on the sale of violent video games to minors in California. In the decision that rejected the case, Justice Antonin Scalia wrote that the link between real-world violence and video games "has been rejected by every court to consider them, and with good reason: They do not prove that violent video games cause minors to act aggressively."[5]

However, some kids are more susceptible to the effects of visual violence (perhaps because of a greater sensitivity, a less agreeable personality, a tendency to be less conscientious than their peers, or even a genetic emotional disorder). Repeated exposure to that kind of content can eventually show up in behavior. Be wise and aware of your child's temperament and your teen becoming calloused toward violence. Overexposure may lead to a lack of empathy and compassion to real victims of violence.

Behavior. Though the connection between video-game violence and real-world violence is tenuous, there are reasons to believe that video games can encourage violence and anger even without showing it on the screen. Video games are designed to light up our brain's reward centers by offering continuous challenges, giving a little hit of dopamine with every success. If we aren't careful, this can result in impulsiveness, impatience, and irritability when gaming is interrupted. Yeah, when you tell them to stop playing and come to the dinner table, your kids aren't exactly in the best mood, right? Although many games can have positive messages or create space for otherwise shy teens to connect with their peers, there is also a danger of your kids slipping into a video game-induced coma for the day without any human contact.

Costs. Money spent on video game titles, consoles, accessories, and in-game purchases of added content can add up fast. Newly released titles can run upwards of $60 each, not to mention the hundreds of dollars you could spend updating tech. Many games are "free," but they make their money from upgrades you buy as you get sucked into (I mean "advance") to a deeper level.

Video games get better, brighter, and more complex with every passing month, and gamers often feel motivated to keep up with the latest trends—not unlike the desire to grab the newest model of an iPhone or trade in an old car for a new one. It's virtually impossible to keep up with every appealing option game companies can offer.

How Can I Keep My Teen's Gaming Healthy?

As you probably guessed, we encourage you not to run from gaming or condemn it, but to engage it. It can be a tool to connect with your teen's heart and teach wisdom. Here are some recommendations.

Take an interest. Most parents don't know much about video games. Show your teen that you care about their interests and teach them self-regulation at the same time by getting involved, watching, learning, and even playing alongside them.

You can search YouTube for any game title and watch promotional trailers and sample gameplay for every game on every console and platform. Watch your teen interact with others during multiplayer games: Is your teen a leader? A follower? The peacemaker? A team-builder? Strategist? Determining these aspects of their personality might help in discovering other activities at which they might excel. Ask them to explain their favorite game to you while you watch.

Ask questions before making judgments: "What do you like best about this game?" "How do you relate to this character?" "Is the story realistic or more fantasy?" "Who in your group of friends is the best player at this game and why?" "How does playing this game make you feel?"

Show your teen how games are made. Explore together the technical/creative aspects of game production, methodology, storyboarding, soundtrack and sound, marketing, voice-over talent—the whole deal. You can even encourage them to create their own game; applications and software for game development are affordable and easy to learn. Your child's hobby could turn into a career path.

Model healthy online habits. Teens are hypersensitive to hypocrisy; we cannot set a standard for them that we won't follow ourselves. Setting up consistent rules for our own screen time will show our teens that we mean what we say. Encourage your whole family to prioritize face-to-face communication where possible. Set up times and spaces where phones, games, and computers don't enter, and protect them. We can't convince our kids that there's value in real-life relationships if we don't live it out ourselves.[6]

Teach internet safety. Remind your kids never to reveal personal information or any details about themselves or your family to anyone online, not even friends they know, since it is easy for others to listen in. They should never arrange to meet someone in person whom they first met online without a trusted adult present. Teens and parents also need to beware of chat in general; even in seemingly innocent games, trolls abound.

Allow your teen to participate in setting limits. Of course, you will make the final decisions, but by discussing them with your teen and hearing their preferences and concerns, you send them a message of respect and give them the opportunity to show maturity. Ask, "What limits do your friends have on their gaming time?" "How long do you think it is appropriate to play at one sitting?" "What kinds of game content could be a problem and why?" "How can you tell when you've played too much?" "How will you avoid letting the game's content seep into your life and attitude?"

Learn to play the game with your teen. Yes, really. Learn to play your teen's favorite games. Ask them to teach you how to use those crazy controllers, and then let them humiliate you at first. Ask for tips and advice. Get better at it. Tell them stories about lining up quarters in the arcade when you were a teen (I know, ancient history). You'll love it. So will they.

Create a no-go list. No one is suggesting you put away your morals in favor of your children's pleasures. Determine what your nonnegotiables are and communicate them clearly: "No playing video games in your bedroom." "No mature-rated video games in our home." "Finish homework and chores before playing any games." "If you get so upset with the game that you throw the controller or lose your temper, you must stop playing immediately." "When I say, 'Get off the game,' do it without griping."

Video games can offer a stress-reliever for the daily pressures of growing up, but they should never substitute for real coping skills. Ensure that your son or daughter is not gaming instead of properly dealing with what's bothering them: bullying, difficulty making friends or relating to teachers, discipline problems at school, or even emerging mood disorders such as anxiety or depression. It's easy to develop a gaming dependency or addiction.

Stronger intervention or limits may also be in order if your teen:

- Seems preoccupied with video gaming—they become distracted or irritable when they aren't playing or talk exclusively about gaming.

- Plays in secret, lies about their gaming time, hides how much they play, or makes excuses to play longer.

- Shows an increase in aggressive behavior or quotes offensive lines learned from a game or a fellow gamer.

- Displays a lack of control, i.e., intends to play for twenty minutes but actually plays for hours. Video games are literally built for this, but so is social media.

- Neglects responsibilities or relationships, including friend-ships, family gatherings, homework, personal hygiene, or other important parts of their lives.
- Spends a majority of their money on video gaming or con-tinually adds upgrades and downloadable content to the games they own.
- Seems unconcerned or defensive about people in their life feeling ignored, left out, or forgotten.

In this next section we will give a brief introduction to some popular gaming trends. This is not exhaustive, just a brief intro-duction to each. For a full analysis of these games and others, download our parent guides for each game at Axis.org.

What Is Discord?

According to their website, it's an "all-in-one voice and text chat for gamers that's free, secure, and works on both your desktop and phone." Basically, it's a way to chat specifically with other gamers about video games (though it's not limited to that). According to their description on the iOS app store:

> Discord is the only cross-platform voice and text chat app designed specifically for gamers. With the iOS app you can stay connected to all your Discord voice and text channels even while AFK [away from keyboard, a common PC gaming slang term]. It is perfect for chatting with team members, seeing who is playing online, and catching up on text conversations you may have missed.

The app works on iPhone, iPad, Android, Mac, and PC and can be used in tandem with all sorts of video games, including mobile games.

According to the company, as of May 2017 they had 45 million active users and had doubled that number to 90 million by the end of the year. They attribute this growth in part to their ability to solve a major communication problem that PC gamers had. Discord created a user-friendly, intuitive, beautiful, and free solution.

Think of Discord itself as a massive lunchroom at school with 90 million students (of any age). The lunchroom is filled with tables around which students congregate in order to talk with each other. These tables are called "servers" and are typically built around a certain game, interest, or group of people. Users can hop from server to server easily, just like a student can move from table to table with ease. (But what a Discord user can do that a real person cannot is look different in each server they're part of.) People at tables can talk one-on-one. These are called "Direct Messages" and cannot be overheard/read by others in the server.

While Discord solves many problems and even makes communication easier and more fun, it brings to the table interesting problems—some seen throughout the internet and some entirely unique. We need to know about these issues not only to protect our kids, but also to utilize them in our efforts to disciple our kids into wise, Christlike, loving citizens of our increasingly virtual world.

Here's what people think is great about Discord:

It's free.

It's quality.

Tons of people can play it.

It's cool and fun.

It builds community and enables communication.

Its platform can be used in other ways.

As with any platform, teens will find all kinds of other creative and harmful uses for it. It doesn't have to live up to its name, but there are plenty of dangers associated with it. You can dig into this at a much deeper level in our *A Parent's Guide to Discord*.

What Is Fortnite?

It's a game in which you move around building "forts" and killing the others until there is only one player left. It is a multiplayer sandbox survival game. "Sandbox" refers to the fact that, in contrast to the progressive story line of many video games, players are put in an open world with few limitations. Instead of completing a level and moving on to the next one, in a sandbox game, players have free access to the world, can change it, and complete challenges within it. (Minecraft is also a sandbox game.)

Survival video games typically put the players in an antagonistic setting, hence the challenge to survive. When Fortnite was originally released, the premise was that a global storm had killed off most of the human population and those who are left must defend themselves against zombies. Players team up and complete missions, constructing traps and defenses against the oncoming horde.

Fortnite is massive. It has a minimum of 45 million players and more than three million concurrent players. Popular among both kids and adults, this game is pulling in hundreds of millions of dollars every month. The game's creators have successfully targeted women as part of their audience: Almost half of Fortnite players are female. Hundreds of thousands of viewers can watch live battles.

In 2017 the battle royale game PlayerUnknown's Battlegrounds (PUBG) was released with widespread success. In response, Epic Games quickly created a battle royale version of Fortnite. The battle royale version of Fortnite has taken the world by storm (no pun intended).

In Fortnite: Battle Royale, participants begin on a hot-air balloon bus and parachute onto an island with up to 99 other players. Each player begins with a pickaxe and a standard parachute and must collect weapons, building materials, and other loot upon landing. They must then defend themselves against attacks from other players as the global storm periodically shrinks. Players who fail to stay within the eye of the storm will die. The last player or squad (team) standing has the honor of achieving the "victory royale."

The game is available on Windows, Mac, Playstation 4, Xbox, Nintendo Switch, and iOS.

The "battle royale" genre of video games is a PvP (player versus player) scenario in which gamers try to kill each other until there is only one survivor. It's basically *The Hunger Games* (minus the evil government)—although the genre gets its name from *Battle Royale*, a 2000 Japanese film in which the government forces a group of ninth graders to fight to the death. There are multiple battle royale video games, and they have become so trendy that other companies are coming out with their own versions of the genre.

People love Fortnite for many reasons:

It offers a free game (while still raking in the money on upgrades).

It offers battle royale style.

There's a low barrier of entry.

It allows for cross-platform play.

Game creators listen to the audience and fix problems.

The visuals and building elements are unique.

Creators understand the power of narrative.

Fortnite has made quite a stir (and a lot of money in the process), but if you engage with your teen about it wisely, it presents opportunities for connection.

What Is Minecraft?

Remember when you really liked playing with Legos before you stepped on them incessantly? The possibilities seemed endless. Nowadays, kids have digital Legos where the possibilities are truly endless. They have Minecraft.

It's a video game that lets users explore, create, and share unique digital worlds filled with resources to gather and monsters to evade or destroy. Like Fortnite, Minecraft is a sandbox game. It encourages users to wander across a nearly infinite digital landscape filled with objects they can turn into resources—trees can be chopped down to become wood, stone can be mined to produce iron—which can then be crafted into items from weapons to houses.

Though the most recent versions do have a price tag ($27 for desktop, $20 for consoles, $7 for mobile), it's possible to access Minecraft: Classic, the original game, for free, although it is no longer updated. It can be accessed on computers, consoles, gaming devices, and phones.

The game offers five modes: Survival, Adventure, Creative, Spectator, and Multiplayer.

Survival: After selecting a difficulty setting (ranging from "peaceful" to "hardcore"), the player spawns inside an unexplored world. Unlike many video games, the player isn't tasked with specific missions in order to proceed; the only goal is to stay alive, a task that involves seeking out food and shelter and crafting weapons to guard against a wide variety of monsters that roam the virtual world when night falls. (Minecraft cycles from day to night every twenty minutes or so.) Depending on the difficulty level, the player might be free to roam around with very few concerns—or they might be desperately trying to find food so their character doesn't die of starvation.

Creative: A player receives unlimited freedom to customize their virtual world; they can summon resources such as brick, flint, and iron at will, then use them to construct whatever they desire—from scale models of the Winter Palace or a space shuttle to a rendering of *Lord of the Rings*' Minas Tirith to a fully functional cell phone inside the game.

Spectator: In this mode, the player acts like a ghost, able to pass through solid objects and view gameplay in real time but without directly interacting. If this sounds silly, try to think of it in the same terms you would a sporting event or a concert: The appeal is seeing artistry on display and maybe picking up something you can try for yourself.

Multiplayer: Exactly what it says: Multiple players gather in a single landscape to show off their skills against one another. However, unlike many multiplayer games, there's no set goal; players interact, collaborate, and build in a shared world, with optional settings allowing them to engage in player-versus-player combat. In multiplayer mode, players are incentivized to develop a culture about how to respect one another's space—an important norm when everyone on the server has the power to kick down the virtual sandcastle others have poured hours of work into.

The online communities can be concerning. Because Minecraft has an online multiplayer option, kids have opportunities to wander into internet neighborhoods you wouldn't consider particularly appropriate and may encounter other users that their parents wouldn't approve of.

Minecraft serves as a creative outlet for kids who feel driven to imagine things. We must never forget that our creativity is a direct connection with our original Creator: Imagining new things and working to bring those ideas to fruition is an act of worship.

What Is Twitch.tv?

Twitch.tv is one of the largest communities on the internet and the most popular eSports streaming service in the world. As the internet's de facto home for the phenomenon of video game streaming, Twitch.tv has fulfilled the dream of millions of middle schoolers: "professional video gamer" is now a legitimate career choice. All they need is a webcam, some software, and a reasonably entertaining personality.

Think of Twitch as a cousin of YouTube, with a specific focus on video games. The site hosts streamers, who film themselves playing games (though the site has expanded to include music shows and painting). Viewers can watch the stream in real time or on demand on their desktops, laptops, smartphones, gaming consoles, or media players like Roku and Amazon Fire. They can also pay to subscribe to channels they particularly like.

Twitch rose to viral prominence in 2014 with Twitch Plays Pokémon, a stream in which viewers collaboratively played Pokémon Red using chat commands. Since then, Twitch.tv has grown steadily to become the fourth largest source of internet traffic during peak periods.

New viewers will often land either on the Twitch home page or on the page of a particular streamer. The home page showcases previews of the live streams that are currently most popular. (Some of the most popular streams will have mature content, but don't worry—those won't be previewed without the user's permission.) From there, they select a live stream of their game, where they will find different live channels of the game and upcoming events.

This is where things can get tricky; it's hard to know just from a preview whether a stream will be family friendly or not. Twitch has specific content guidelines about what kinds of games can be streamed (sexually explicit content is high on the banned list), but salty language is fairly common among streamers. In addition, a broadcaster can indicate if a channel is intended for mature audiences, at which point a viewer will have to click on "Start Watching" before viewing the stream.

Finally, when viewing a stream, there will always be a chat window, which can be overwhelmingly quick and contain inappropriate language. This window starts populating as soon as one joins a stream, regardless of whether one has clicked "Start Watching" on a mature stream or not. Be aware of toxic comment sections, lax content moderation, sexually themed content, and the risk of screen addiction. It's up to us as parents to teach our children how to navigate this new landscape in a healthy, God-honoring way.

Is my kid just watching other people play video games? Yes and no. In one sense, Twitch is *Monday Night Football* for the new millennium, with competitors wearing headsets instead of helmets. But though viewers and subscribers are technically only watching someone else play video games, it's not all they come for; they're really there for the experience.

As with YouTube and the now-defunct Vine, Twitch streamers attract (and depend on) viewers for their channels to thrive, but Twitch's monetized subscription model and the intimacy of live-streaming has taken the phenomenon to new levels. Subscriptions ostensibly pay for customizable emoticons and other small upgrades to the viewers' experience, but the real draw is a sense of community. Viewers share in the thoughts, inside jokes, victories, and disappointments of their streamers; subscribing to support them is a way to make the relationship more real.

Twitch has some broad content guidelines for their communities, but by and large, the content will depend on the stream. If you're not comfortable letting your kids see or hear explicit language, it may be wise to watch a stream yourself for fifteen minutes or so to get an idea of just what kind of content you should expect. If the streamer is appropriate but the chat is not, there is an option to turn on "hide chat" in the Twitch settings. This sense of community is most acute with streamers, but Twitch also makes big events, like Comic-Con and PAX, accessible to viewers thousands of miles away.

What Is League of Legends?

League of Legends, aka League or LoL, is a vastly popular game and has remained so since its introduction in 2009. League of Legends is the biggest video game in the world: It sports more than 100 million monthly players, with at least 27 million of those playing daily. Beyond that, competitive LoL play is also becoming as massively popular as many traditional sports. League team infrastructure is starting to look more like franchises from the NFL or NBA. It even has its own ESPN page and has been in conversations with the Olympic Committee about the possibility of e-sports in the Olympics. In addition, LoL offers salaries to pro players, with some making as much as Major League Soccer players.

It's understandable why your teen would want to play it, but they need guidance, wisdom, training, and boundaries in order to learn how to use it well and keep it from consuming their life. Whether your child has been playing LoL for years or has just downloaded the game for the first time, this guide will help you better understand the world of League so you can disciple them.

While the game is free, the creators have monetized the snot out of it. When starting a game, teams of five are formed (either known friends/players or random players picked by the game). Then each player picks their character/champion for that game. The object of the game is to defeat the other team by destroying their "Nexus" hidden inside and protected by their base. To do that, players start in their home base on one side of the map. Between the two bases are three paths or "lanes." Each player starts with a few items and healing potions, collecting more over the course of the game to aid them as they go out into their lanes, face opposing champions, kill minions, and take down defensive towers. Little accomplishments also earn them experience and gold, both of which make them stronger and help them gain more abilities essential for winning the game. As more towers fall, the map becomes much more open, and players can roam more freely, which eventually prompts a team battle. Whichever team gains the edge and destroys the Nexus wins. An evenly matched game takes between twenty and sixty minutes. There are currently three game modes that provide subtle changes to the conditions and rules of play.

League is a multiplayer online battle arena (MOBA) rated T for Teen and is compatible with both Windows and Mac OS systems, and it can now be played on a smartphone, both Android and iPhone.

Strategy: A player's decisions have a significant impact on the outcome of the game, rather than strength being the main factor, like Risk or chess. Situational awareness is particularly important in these games, and for League that means being aware of both your immediate situation and the larger arena map.

Action Real-Time Strategy (ARTS, aka MOBA, Multiplayer Online Battle Arena): In contrast to the turn-by-turn play of Risk, LoL allows you to take actions at any time. Imagine chess without turns, where you can move any of your pieces as fast as you're able—but then again, so can your opponent. The RTS element requires fast thinking and high levels of focus and engagement.

Team Based: Coordination, cooperation, and playmaking are necessary to fully combat the opposing team. On each team there are five different roles, each having their own part to play, kind of like the positions in baseball. Each position is played differently and adds much variety to the gameplay. Communication skills also come into play when interacting with other players.

Role Playing Game (RPG): This is any game in which you assume the role of a character, either by acting and speaking as them or by developing them with your decisions (Dungeons & Dragons is also an RPG). League is an RPG thanks to its champions, which have extensive backstories, origin stories, character development, and key virtues or vices. This doesn't have much to do with the game play, but it's there if players choose to delve into it.

People love League for many reasons:

There are many possibilities because its creators work hard to make it appeal to many types of players.

There is a low barrier to entry because it's free and it matches you with opponents of similar skill levels.

It's constantly being improved and updated with new champions and play styles.

It offers the ability to play casually with friends or battle for prestige in ranked tournaments.

You can watch professionals battle it out in the world championships every year, complete with a specialized stadium, close to 60 million online viewers, opening ceremonies, and a big shiny trophy. (Fun fact: The 2017 League of Legends World Championship, held in the sold-out Bird's Nest Arena in Beijing, China, was the most-watched gaming event in history to date.)

Like the other games and platforms, it has dangers and has some intricate things you need to know about it. Download our *A Parent's Guide to League of Legends* for a full explanation.

Engaging in Video Games with Wisdom

It's easy for teens or adults to fall into unhealthy habits with games. They're literally designed to be addictive. We crave the dopamine release associated with accomplishments, and video games offer continuous hits. And, as with many addictive behaviors, video game addiction can often arise as a symptom of deeper problems—loneliness, dissatisfaction, purposelessness, and others.

Because addiction often serves as a salve to the feeling of disconnection, it's important not to make your teen feel attacked or devalued when you broach the topic of their habit. Ease into it. Express an interest in their favorite games. Show them that you care about them and, by extension, the things they care about. With that foundation, you can start having conversations about what the habit is doing to them, and how they can regain control without abandoning something they feel is a part of their identity. Encourage your teen to pursue games in a healthy way that honors themselves and God without cutting themselves off from community. It's possible to spend a reasonable amount of time on their hobby without losing the ability to engage with the people around them. Don't just talk about the act or habit or video games, engage with your teen's heart in your conversations.

12

College

If ours is an examined faith, we should be unafraid of doubt. If doubt is eventually justified, we were believing what clearly was not worth believing. But if doubt is answered, our faith has grown stronger.

Os Guiness

Your first 72 hours on campus are the most important hours of your college career. The choices you make in terms of friends, peer groups, and using your free time will heavily determine how well you will navigate your college course.

InterVarsity[1]

You doubt because you love the truth.

George MacDonald, *Lilith*

I (David) heard a story that grieved me to the core. At a major state university freshman orientation, they passed around a basket of condoms with the flippant warning to have safe sex and make sure the other person is consenting. They made a bigger deal of sex than learning. The main point of college orientation: Don't rape anyone. Is this really a moral guide?

Remember my friends from the high school mission trip? One is dead. Many of them are divorced. One of them is really successful, but only gets to see his kids every other week. I watched friends go to college and struggle. The parties sucked them in. The wondering slipped into wandering. This makes me sad and angry.

I watched three culprits go unchecked and lead friends away from their faith: culture, partying, and professors. I watched friends cannonball into the deep end during and after college. Those four years had an inordinate effect on their lives. If you don't disciple your kids, our culture will. If you don't orient them with a compasss, our culture and college will toss them another compass.

College is a confusing conundrum. Is it forming young people or deforming them? The answer is yes. What started as a clever plan for efficient education has spiraled into a much bigger idea. For some it has become a nightmare. The immense pressure to succeed and set themselves up for their future can lead to extreme anxiety that is fed by little sleep and aided by drugs like Adderall. Some exit their college years with wounds and debt that may last a lifetime. College is portrayed in shows and movies as a free-for-all full of parties, sex, drugs, and an unlimited supply of good times. College is glorified as an escape, a four-year retreat, not a chance to invest in your future. For many, college is the ultimate in "overpromise and underdeliver."

Remember, the smartphone is seen as the new university. You can learn anything you want to! On this magical device you can take courses from experts at your own pace. You can binge a podcast and learn a new skill by tomorrow. You can consume "how to" YouTube videos incessantly and learn the new tactics faster than ever. This is both awesome and scary at the same time, but it's changing how we view college. Expensive higher education is no longer an assumed value in middle-class culture as it was for boomers and Gen Xers. The conversation about the value of it will continue to morph.

While your kids are saying goodbye to old friends and stressing over how to decorate their dorm rooms, you will be much more realistic, fretting about keggers, atheist professors, coed dorms, and the allure of total freedom. Ultimately, as our children leave home and our loving boundaries for the first time, we're concerned about a much more important question: *How do I help my kids keep their faith in college?*

More than being concerned about statistics or behaviors, we want them to choose to follow Christ because they know that doing so is the only way to find abundant life, both now and for eternity. But we know that colleges and universities can be places where other promises of happiness, success, love, and satisfaction compete voraciously to win their hearts and minds. So we begin to wonder: *Did we do enough? What can we do before they leave? And what can we do once they're there?*

Don't Panic

We know that this transition can be terrifying, but we want to encourage you in two things. First, colleges typically aren't as hostile as we see in movies, and second, challenges and new environments can (and often do) help deepen faith, as long as teens have the right place to go to ask questions and get guidance. So rather than dreading this time, remember that it's really good for them to be tested a little. With the right connections and resources, your child can emerge from college with a deeper faith than they started with.

We know the statistics can be a little intimidating. But we need to take them for what they are: *just* numbers. Your child is not defined by a number, and God is bigger than the statistics.

With that in mind, Fuller Youth Institute found that 40 to 50 percent of students walk away from the church after they graduate from high school.[2] And according to the Public Religion Research Institute, 38 percent of young adults are religiously unaffiliated, compared with 24 percent of all Americans.[3] And here's the kicker: Most of the young adults who walk away from God or their faith actually do so *before* leaving for college.[4] This shows that the assumption that colleges destroy faith isn't true. We can't oversimplify the situation and say, "*If* my teen goes to college, *then* they're going to lose their faith." The issue is more complicated, which leaves a lot of room for opportunity, hope, and the Holy Spirit.

Whether or not our teens graduate with their faith intact depends on two things: God and their own hearts. We need to free ourselves from the expectation that if we don't do everything right, our kids are bound to walk away. The converse can also be damaging when we think if we do everything right, they won't walk away. Remember, Adam and Eve had the perfect Father but ultimately chose to rebel against him.

It's not ultimately up to us, because our kids are their own people with free will, but there are definitely steps we can take to prepare them well. Just keep in mind that God deeply knows the heart of your child, and he's guiding them through every phase of life, including college. There are awesome opportunities for Christian community on just about every college campus, but it may take a little bit of elbow grease from you and your child to find the right one. So don't lose heart! We're only getting started, and we've got some tips for setting your teen up for success in their faith.

Will Going to a Christian College Help?

Maybe. But there are so many factors at play—your child's personality, the schools themselves, your child's friends, costs, whether their field of study is offered at a school, etc.—it's impossible to say for sure, so it's worth considering and talking about with your child. Things like community, quality of education, location, and cost are important, but it's possibly more important to assess where your child is at in their faith and if they're ready to represent Christ to those at a non-Christian school or if they need more time in a safe environment to ask questions, experience Jesus, and allow their faith to solidify.

Keep in mind that choosing a school *for* your child is not necessarily a good way to make sure they keep their faith. For example, if your teenager wants to go to a non-Christian school because they like the freedoms it offers but you force them to go to a Christian school anyway, they will still find ways to do those things at the Christian school. If our kids want to do (or not do) something, they'll find a way. So when talking with your teenager about his/her future, remember that asking them about what they hope for and dream about can be more effective in getting them to think beyond the short-term fun or happiness they're currently pursuing.

One of the biggest draws for Christian schools is the faith aspect, of course. A 2005 study of 16,000 students found that those who attend independent Protestant, Baptist, and other Protestant-affiliated institutions report the largest increases in overall religious commitment. This is encouraging because, if our kids choose to attend a Christian school, we would hope that the school would ultimately deepen their faith, not eliminate it.

Besides the curriculum, chapels, and Christian professors, your teen will also enjoy the presence of strong community. This is not to say that friendships are guaranteed to form on day one and never break—we're all human, of course. Everyone can have a little bit of trouble finding the right community, whether it's in a Christian atmosphere or not. But at a school where everyone shares a common belief, it can be easier to build friendships because those like-minded people are all over the campus.

This is all good news! But here are a few other points to keep in mind.

- Not all Christian universities are created equal. Many are Christian in name but not in action or philosophy. Speak with alumni and admissions staff to find out if this is true.
- Like churches, Christian schools often follow denominations. It's worth finding a school that's transparent about its theology, but also encourages depth of thought over blind agreement.
- Christian schools often have mandatory chapel attendance or some other equivalent. There are pros and cons to this situation, but know that just because a college offers Christian resources such as chaplains, prayer, and service opportunities, this doesn't mean your teen will pursue them.
- The Christian bubble does exist. We need to encourage our kids to step outside of that bubble and become Christ's ambassadors to the world around them.

What about Public Schools?

Attending a non-religious college can have just as much of a positive impact on students' faith as a Christian school. The Chronicle Review, published by the *Chronicle of Higher Education*, states that attending public school as a Christian tends to strengthen the faith of a student, while Bible schools may not actually be the healthiest environment for growth. Part of the reason is that at public schools (more so than at Christian schools), it's almost guaranteed that students' beliefs will be challenged, requiring them to think more deeply and actively wrestle with their faith.

If your child wishes to attend a public school, there are plenty of opportunities to pursue the Christian faith through clubs, Bible studies, and churches; all your teen has to do is be willing to try them out. Try looking into some Christian clubs with your teen before he or she leaves for college so that they have a good idea of what's out there. InterVarsity, Young Life, Cru, and the Navigators are national organizations that are available on most campuses, but make sure to look into campus-specific ministries and clubs as well. Check into denominations and core values to make sure you find the right fit for your child.

A cool part of pursuing Christianity on a campus full of different beliefs is that we can know our students made a genuine choice to follow God on their own. God gave us free will for a reason, and he wants your child to exercise it on their college campus. Faith in Christ is a choice, one we each have to make for ourselves; we can't force our kids into a faith they don't want. Part of letting them go in their college journey is allowing them to explore God's love for themselves.

In Romans 12:2, Paul reminds us to not conform to the world, but to be transformed by the renewal of our minds. Paul lived in a world filled with different beliefs, but he didn't run from it; he stayed in it, engaging it in order to show Jesus' love to all. Jesus set this example when he ate with tax collectors and was anointed by a sinful woman, demonstrating the importance of being *in* the world but not *of* it. However, we'd be remiss if we overlooked the temptations that can be much more widespread and pervasive at non-Christian schools. If our children's faith isn't yet mature or they seem easily swayed by culture, college could be a place where their faith isn't refined, but completely eradicated. As the parent, you have the best perspective to know if your child is ready to be in the world without becoming of it, or if they need more time in a less hostile environment.

What Pressures Will My Kid Experience in College?

Relationship pressures: According to the Fuller Youth Institute, only one in seven high school seniors feels prepared to face the challenges of college life.[5] It's "the perfect storm of loneliness, the search for new friends, being completely on their own for the first time, and the sudden availability of a lot of partying."[6] These factors tend to stress parents out even more than the kids, but they're not doomed, we promise. While parties and alcohol might be intriguing, if your teen doesn't have a desire to participate in those things, they really don't have to. A lot of kids go into college believing that they have to conform to cultural norms in order to fit in, but it's just not the case. There are numerous groups and lots of people who find meaning outside of those things, they just need to explore what the school has to offer. Talk to your teen about what they'd like to be a part of socially and help them find organizations that fit those interests. It's critical that they get connected in their first two weeks of being on campus because, as Dr. Kara Powell says, "The first two weeks of college set the trajectory" for the rest of their experience.[7]

Academic pressures: Aside from social pressures, many students find academics to be highly taxing. A national study from New York University found that 55 percent of students said academics were their biggest stressor.[8] This pressure can lead to a deep sense of anxiety. And while academics and learning are important, we need to remind our kids that their value is not rooted in or determined by a grade. College curriculum is a major shift from high school, and some students struggle with it more than others. So before your child leaves for school, talk to them about the importance of having a good balance in their life. Encourage them to study hard but not place their ultimate value in a grade.

College classes are tough, and students don't need straight As to be successful. Those who went through school getting those straight As may be shocked that they're not getting the same results in college, but the national average for college students is actually a 3.15, or a B average.[9] We parents can have a hard time with this sometimes because we just want to see our kids do the absolute best they can. But it's important to watch our posture with them, especially when it comes to academics.[10] Remind your teen or college student of important things like, "Grades don't determine your worth," and "I can see that you're working hard, and I'm so proud of you."

They will constantly be dealing with fear of failure, judgment, and the feeling of letting you down. Remind them that they haven't disappointed you and that you're immensely proud of them. When our kids know that we love and support them no matter what, they can relax and possibly do better without the burden of pressure and expectation weighing them down. We've seen that college students can become so overwhelmed by the pressures of life that their faith takes a back seat. College exposes and agitates deep emotional and social needs, and students often try to fill those needs with friends, activities, and parties. Thus, faith falls by the wayside simply because students are so eager to find some shred of comfort and acceptance.

Fear of failure: There are so many fears swirling around high school and college students with roots in the fear of failure. The fear of not getting good grades, the future after graduation, trying out for teams or parts, and failing to make friends are colliding. Help them learn to regulate and take care of themselves by cultivating practices such as going to the gym, reading (for fun), playing sports, and pursuing their hobbies. Teach them about the faith aspect of rest. God gave us unique ways to cope with stress, and it's essential to participate in those things to maintain our own sanity. Because, while many students will turn to partying to let go, we want to remind our kids that there is so much more available to us.

What about Professors?

Chances are, if your teen attends a public school, there will be professors who come from non-Christian worldviews. But this does not mean that all professors are out to destroy your child's faith. In fact, most professors actually tend to encourage individual thought and opinions.

Statistics aren't as concerning as we might have thought. In 2007, *Harvard Magazine* wrote, "Although nearly 37 percent of professors at elite research schools like Harvard are atheist or agnostic, about 20 percent of their colleagues have 'no doubt that God exists.' At community colleges, in contrast, 15 percent of professors are atheist or agnostic, and 40 percent believe in God."[11]

Most professors want to see their students succeed, regardless of their religious beliefs. For many, that's why they've chosen this profession. Some professors might make snarky comments about religion or conservative values. While they might not be actively fighting against religion, professors' subtle disdain might suggest to your teen that "smart" people don't believe in God. But that's clearly not true, and we can help our children by reminding them that beliefs shouldn't change based on what others think of us, but rather be based on truth.

In fact, perspective is everything here. If our kids go into college afraid of anyone who might question their faith, they'll see any such experience as negative and as an attack. But if, as we read in James 1:2–4 ESV, they "count it all joy, my brothers, when you meet trials of various kinds, for you know that the testing of your faith produces steadfastness. And let steadfastness have its full effect, that you may be perfect and complete, lacking in nothing," then they'll see such experiences as opportunities to learn, grow, and possibly even help others examine their own beliefs.

It's actually a *really good thing* for our kids to be exposed to different religions, worldviews, and philosophies. We can't expect to keep our kids in a protective Christian bubble for the rest of their lives. Sooner or later, they'll have friends who hold contrasting beliefs, start a discussion with a coworker on the meaning of life, or see a protest sign that promotes a different view. The point is this: If Christianity is true, it will stand up to scrutiny, questions, attacks, and mockery.

Therefore, it's good to ask hard questions and think deeply about our faith in pursuit of what is good, true, and real. Then, when we encounter people with different beliefs and values, we won't be afraid of them; rather, we'll be able to rest in our faith and have calm, respectful conversations with them.

Drinking and Sex in College

Yes, both are prevalent on most campuses, even Christian campuses. (As of 2016, 57.2 percent of college students said they drank in the last month, 38 percent engaged in binge drinking in the past month, and 10.5 percent were heavy drinkers).[12] It's easy to imagine worst-case scenarios, which compounds the fear and worry, often leading us to want to tighten the reins so we prevent these scenarios from becoming reality. And while it's good to have honest, open dialogue with teens about the dangers of binge drinking, driving while intoxicated, sexual assault, and more, it's never helpful to try to control our kids.

Remember, they are their own people with free will to make their own decisions. So once they go to college, it's important to trust that you did everything you could while they were in your home to empower them to become thoughtful, mature, Christ-oriented, responsible adults. Even more important, rest in the knowledge that the Creator of the universe loves your child more than you can comprehend and is always working to bring their heart closer to his.

With that said, it's not the end of the world if they go to a party or drink alcohol. *What? But parties are where evil itself is manifested!* Don't hear what we're not saying: We don't condone underage drinking, drinking to drunkenness, or putting oneself in risky situations. But because this is the first time many of our kids will be on their own and in full control of their decisions, they will probably test the waters here and there. Rather than freaking out or taking it as an opportunity to remind them (again) of how terrible partying is, take a deep breath, resist the urge to react emotionally, and ask them about the experience. One more reminder to put on your "I'm not shocked" face. You want them to feel safe enough to be honest with you, at which point you can guide them with good questions toward a healthy, reality-based perspective of how those choices will affect them in the long term. In addition, let them know you trust them to make the right choices. When we say, "Don't drink, don't go out, and don't make poor choices," our kids hear, "I don't trust you to make the right choices, so I'm telling you what you should do instead." Do we intend this interpretation? Of course not! We want our kids to be safe, and our cautionary tales are coming from a place of love, but we need to extend them the respect they're craving. In addition, it's much more powerful to gently and lovingly guide our kids to the truth than to spoon-feed it to them.

As you have these conversations, two important things to keep in mind are that even the best kids are not perfect, and we need to talk to them as adults, not helpless kids.

Talk through your own experiences with college parties. Did you drink or engage in risky behavior? Be real with your kids; let them know that you've been there and that you are available to talk.

Create a space for vulnerability so that your kids can feel free to come to you if they need help.

Drinking can also lead to a higher chance of sexual assault. Though it is not inevitable, there is often a direct correlation between drinking and sexual assault; many assaults on college campuses involve alcohol.

The search for intimacy through pleasure and alcohol can lead to risky situations, and those can lead to extremely traumatic events, including sexual assault. Again, alcohol will not inevitably result in an assault, but it is more likely to occur when guards are down and vulnerability sets in. When talking with your child about this, let him or her know the risks of assault in conjunction with alcohol, but state clearly that alcohol is never an excuse for assault. Sexual assault is not the fault of the victim, whether drinking was involved or not. The role of alcohol is simply something to be aware of, because when inhibitions are stripped away, the risks can increase quickly.[13]

Sex is openly discussed at most US colleges. Modern culture advocates for sex as long as it's "safe" and "healthy," i.e., both parties are consenting and use protection. So it's likely that the student body will be pretty accepting of sexual activity. Many colleges will also present themselves as the authorities on sex. They will likely provide free events and consultations to students who have questions. As parents, we need to let our kids know that there are other authorities to turn to for questions and advice. Talk with your child about how to recognize the culture and live differently. God's design for sex is a beautiful picture of his union with us.

Engage in Conversations about Doubt. Now.

College is often associated with youth doubting their faith. The thought of college scares many Christian parents for this reason alone. Like it or not, we live in an increasingly post-Christian culture that no longer accepts the basic tenets of Christianity as universal truth. The rise of religious pluralism, relativism, and agnostic attitudes toward faith are changing the cultural landscape. Though frustrating, these shifts provide fresh opportunities to engage our children with both the evidence for and the heart of Christianity. Begin preparing your child for college as soon as possible. Getting them to think ahead sooner will give them more time to ask questions and offer you more time to have good conversations with them.

Despite what it may feel like—"I've done something wrong!" "Clearly his faith isn't strong enough!" or "She's just going to walk away from her faith!"—when a teen or preteen starts asking real questions about faith, God, Christianity, and other belief systems, it's nothing to panic about. In fact, it's not only normal but also a very healthy and developmentally appropriate part of spiritual growth. So many of us have echoed these words from Mark 9:24: "I do believe; help me overcome my unbelief!"

If your teen is struggling with questions or doubts, he or she is joining a great cloud of witnesses who've been on the same journey. From John the Baptist, "Doubting Thomas," and Martin Luther to C. S. Lewis and Mother Teresa, Christianity is filled with individuals who intellectually and spiritually struggled to believe, but through their authentic quest they came to a place of deep trust and reliance upon God.

However, in some circles of Christianity, this rich history of doubting well has recently been replaced with a strict adherence to blind faith, ignoring evidence rather than following it, and fearing questions rather than using them to make one's faith stronger. Young Christians were taught to do as they were told, rather than to think for themselves.

The results have been disastrous, with many millennials and Gen Zers choosing to walk away from a belief system that seemed misogynistic, oppressive, illogical, and downright boring. But it absolutely doesn't have to be that way. We believe, like so many generations of Christians before us, that we have nothing to fear from questions, doubts, and scrutiny because the evidence points solidly and firmly to Christ as Risen Savior. We also believe that following and becoming more like him is the only path to true fulfillment, flourishing, and life.

So rather than allowing our teens' curiosity and/or skepticism to scare us, let's breathe, relax, and view this as an opportunity to bring them into the rich history of skeptics who found that Christ was who they'd been looking for all along and to bring them into deep, lifelong flourishing. After all, if God is who he says he is, then no question, doubt, or other barrier to belief is too big for him.

"Tolerance" and relativism: There is so much truth being ignored in the name of tolerance. This flavor of tolerance stems from an attempt to be inclusive and show love and grace, but what results is that anything deemed as "intolerant" (i.e., claiming to know truth or saying that one belief system is correct while another is incorrect) is labeled as hate speech. Teens often hear phrases like, "What's true for you may not be true for me," "That's your truth," or "There is no truth, only perspective." Thus, the entire basis for any belief system comes into question, making it hard for a person to commit to anything that claims to know such things as right and wrong.

Ironically, this postmodern belief self-destructs when applied to itself. To say, "There is no truth," is itself a truth claim. Whenever someone makes a claim like this, simply ask, "Is that true?" By applying the claim to itself, phrases like these are easily shown to be self-defeating and absurd, therefore rendering the postmodern understanding of "tolerance" self-defeating as well.

Instead, real tolerance is agreeing that people have the right to believe whatever they want while understanding that not everything we believe is right. As Christians, we acknowledge that there is truth and that truth is good. The problem with holding tolerance and truth in tension is that to embrace truth, you have to be intolerant of some ideas. You cannot always be all-inclusive. We Christians can and should help others see the flaw in this meaning of tolerance while treating people with gentleness and respect (1 Peter 3:15). We must keep in mind that a person making an absurd claim is not himself absurd. The key is to be inclusive (tolerant) of people, but exclusive (intolerant) of bad/false ideas.

Expect and prepare for questions. You can't teach your kids enough that they'll never doubt. We want to come back to engaging doubt as conversation instead of condemning it or running from it. If your teen is wondering about God, that's good. Talk to them about their doubts. Ask questions. Put on your "I'm not shocked" face.[14] Big faith questions will likely arise before college but expect them to rear their head during college. Expect questions such as, How do we know God is real? How do we know the Bible is true? Did Jesus really rise from the dead? Can we trust the Bible? Is the Bible the Word of God? How do we know what truth is? Is Jesus God? If the universe came from nothing, is there any purpose to anything? Do we have evidence God exists?

Here is a list of questions to begin discussing with your teen:

- What does the Bible mean to you? How has it helped guide you in your daily life? Tell a story about a time you were really thankful for the Bible.
- Who do you think Jesus is? How does your life reflect that?
- How is it good news that Jesus saves us and it isn't up to us to save ourselves? How would the way you talk about God be different if you knew why you believed in him?
- What do you think college life will be like? What are college parties like? What are college professors like? What will the religious and antireligious environment on campus be like?

If we knew of a way to absolutely guarantee that your teen wouldn't walk away from God, we would be screaming it from the rooftops! But alas, there's no such guarantee. Teens may still express doubt even if they know the answers to the most basic questions about Christianity. This is because there are actually three kinds of doubt: intellectual, emotional, and volitional doubt.

Intellectual doubts come from having questions regarding the truth of Christianity. There is a lot to think through and learn.

Emotional doubts are not questions about the evidence as much as feelings that Christianity is untrue. Emotional doubts may stem from a traumatic experience and typically involve questions about the goodness of God or his forgiveness.

Volitional doubt is a doubt of the will. A person experiencing volitional doubt may simply be asking why the evidence of God's existence or goodness matters at all and may tend to be apathetic and not care about the truth. Identifying the kind of doubt your child is experiencing is the first step in determining how to respond because each type of doubt requires different guidance. We must remember that faith isn't merely believing the right things about God, but is also a life of faithfulness toward the God revealed in

Scripture. To limit faith to merely thinking the right things about God and not living them out daily is an impotent faith. Therefore, we must also equip our teenagers to own their faith by living it out. There is no such thing as abstract faith that is not personally embodied in the real world.

Helping teens wrestle with doubt is intimidating. By now I'm sure you know we're going to bring you back to engaging in the lifelong conversation, not running from it. The process often takes time because there are rarely quick fixes or easy answers. Remember not to rush into things. Instead, start by asking good questions. Also, be honest with teens about your own doubts and search out answers together. By leading with vulnerability, you will show your teen that there is space and freedom to question and wrestle with the truth. Their doubts offer parents the opportunity to model God's unending compassion by helping them understand that there is no shame in having doubts. Rest in the fact that your teen's doubts may actually be the first step into a more vibrant, authentic faith that they can call their own and that cannot be "blown here and there by every wind of teaching and by the cunning and craftiness of people in their deceitful scheming" (Ephesians 4:14).

Some Questions about College to Discuss with Your Teen

Motivation: *Why should someone pursue college? Why should someone avoid it?*

Cost: *Approximately how much does it cost? Is it worth it?*

Purpose: *What is college for? How could it help them work toward their dreams and goals?*

Alternatives: *What other educational options are available?*

Expectations: *What are their expectations of college? What are your expectations of them during college?*

Timing: *When is the right time for college? Would a gap year or two help them prepare for college? If so, how?*

13

Depression and Anxiety

It's clear that teens are in the midst of a mental health emergency.

Rich Karlgaard[1]

Take courage; I have overcome the world.

Jesus[2]

Youth is the new global currency.

Simon Doonan

Our team recently spent some time with student pastors to better understand the realities of their role. The most painful thing they described was the horror of getting the call that a student had committed suicide. Rick Warren, pastor of one of the largest evangelical churches in the United States and author of one of the biggest bestsellers in history, *The Purpose-Driven Life*, lost his son to suicide after a long battle with a serious depressive disorder. A quarter of pastors admit to having suffered with a mental illness themselves, and painful stories of pastor suicide hit the news occasionally. Even Winston Churchill suffered terribly from a lifelong, untreated mood disorder he referred to as a "black dog" that would sit on his lap and haunt him.[3]

The numbers are staggering. The epidemic is real. Anxiety, depression, and suicide are on the rise among teens. Let's acknowledge the elephant in the room: *This is a scary topic that no parent wants to even think about.* After all, God created us for flourishing, abundant life and relationship with Him, not pain, sadness, or the desire to no longer live. Unfortunately, our broken world is full of dysfunction, disorder, and sin, all of which disrupt and decay the beautiful world God lovingly created for us.

These are heavy conversations, but we can't afford to avoid them. Depression and suicide are everywhere. Look at the numbers. "Today five to eight times as many high school and college students meet the diagnostic criteria for major depression and/or anxiety disorder as in the 1960s. The Centers for Disease Control recently found that among high school students in the United States, '16 percent reported seriously considering suicide, 13 percent reported creating a plan for suicide, and 8 percent reported trying to take their own life in the 12 months preceding the survey.'"[4]

So what do we do when the teens we love struggle with these issues? How do we help our kids find physical, mental, emotional, and spiritual healing? First, let us assure you that if you or a loved one are struggling, you're not alone. Nearly ten million people in the United States seriously considered suicide during the past twelve months.[5] With the exception of accidents, suicide is the leading cause of death among young adults and teens, but has even affected children as young as age five.[6] And one in five females and one in seven males engage in some type of self-injury each year.[7]

But there is hope. Now more than ever, behavioral health providers are studying and learning about teen mental health issues, and new resources are created every year. We do not pretend to be physicians, healthcare providers, or even experts on these difficult matters; this is an introduction, not a substitute for medical advice or treatment. It can accompany and support actions directed or confirmed by a qualified healthcare professional, but it is not meant to replace or preclude any diagnosis or treatment by a qualified healthcare professional. Axis cannot be responsible for actions taken without professional medical guidance.

We cannot say it loudly enough or often enough: If you even suspect your child has suicidal thoughts or plans, stop reading this and take action now. Contact your family physician and tell them your teen is at risk of suicide and must be seen immediately. If a doctor cannot see them right away for whatever reason, do not leave your child alone until they can be seen and evaluated by a healthcare professional qualified to assess adolescent behavioral health. If necessary, take your child to the nearest emergency room or urgent care center, demand priority, and do not leave until next steps are in place (such as referral to a specialist, assessments, evaluations, treatment plans, outpatient/inpatient programs, etc.).

The Centers for Disease Control define suicide as "death caused by self-injurious behavior with any intent to die as a result of the behavior."[8] Studies report "the majority of young people who attempt suicide have a significant mental health disorder, usually major depression."[9] In the very young, suicide attempts are often impulsive and can be triggered by feelings of sadness, confusion, anger, or problems with attention and hyperactivity. Among teens, suicide attempts may be associated with feelings of stress, self-doubt, pressure to succeed, financial uncertainty, disappointment, and loss.

The idea of ending one's own life is certainly nothing new; it's significantly visible (though not sanctioned) in US culture and even acceptable in other cultures. The ancient Greeks allowed convicted criminals to take their own lives; the ancient Romans did too, at first, until the high incidence of suicide among slaves began to impact the wealth of slave-owners. Spiritual traditions including

Buddhism and Hinduism and countries such as Japan and India view suicide as an acceptable option in particular situations. The concept of suicide appears frequently in visual art, literature, history books, film, and music from around the world. Terrorists and extremist religious groups see suicide as an ideological option for the sake of a cause deemed more significant than individual life, and six US states allow physician-assisted suicide for those suffering from terminal illnesses with a prognosis of fewer than six months to live.

What is self-harm? Self-harm, clinically referred to as "non-suicidal self-injury" or NSSI, is defined as "injury inflicted by a person on him/herself deliberately but without intent to die."[10] Teens today often refer to self-harm as "cutting" since the most common form of self-harm involves cutting the skin with a sharp object, such as a razor or knife. However, there are many forms of self-harm, including burning the skin with cigarettes or other hot objects, pulling hair, hitting oneself or banging one's body against walls, deep fingernail scratching, ingesting low levels of toxins, pinching the skin, or picking at wounds to prevent them from healing.

Why would someone self-harm?

Many assume self-harm signals the presence of a severe mental illness in a teen; after all, who in their right mind would intentionally hurt themselves, right? Self-harming is not an illness in itself but rather points to a desperate situation and a dangerously severe inability to cope—which can be caused by one or any number of physical, mental, emotional, or spiritual issues.

The urge to self-harm, like suicidal ideation, most often begins with overwhelming negative emotions and problems that seem unsolvable. Sometimes a person who continues to struggle with acute depression, emotional pain, or trauma will eventually "go numb": The brain can shut down emotions to protect itself from toxic levels of stress. This automatic neurological response can hold a person hostage inside themselves, preventing them from crying, getting angry, solving problems well, focusing, or even fully understanding what they feel and why. In these frightening moments, self-harm can feel like a "release" in a strange way.

Those who engage in it say they feel "real" and "alive" again because it makes their invisible, unexplainable pain "visible." It can distract a person temporarily from the nonstop internal struggle they live with every day. A few even admit they self-harm in order to stop suicidal thoughts because the painful sensation briefly restores a sense of control over their lives.

What Causes Suicide or Self-Harm?

There isn't a single cause for either behavior, and researchers are unsure what is causing the rates of both to increase. Some align the increase in screen time among teens with their rise in suicidal thoughts. Others say bullying is the culprit. Some point to rising cultural pressures that result in anxiety. Some blame today's parenting styles, a lack of awareness, or the world's values falling apart. There has also been speculation that media are to blame.

In March 2017, the independent television series *13 Reasons Why* explored a teen suicide in a more direct way than a series ever dared before. The show focused on a troubled high school student who recorded audio explanations of what and who influenced her decision to kill herself, then she labeled each tape with the name of a person (a total of 13, hence the title) she felt contributed to the decision. Each episode of the show followed one of these people as they deal with the girl's self-inflicted death and the part they may have played in it. CNN reported that after the pilot episode aired, online search results for terms like "suicide," "suicide prevention," and "suicide awareness" rose significantly. However, search results for the phrases "how to commit suicide" and "suicidal ideation" also skyrocketed. Psychologists call this phenomenon "suicide contagion," when a group's exposure to details of a suicide result in increased suicidal behavior in that group. This can also happen when a celebrity commits suicide, as with Linkin Park singer Chester Bennington's suicide in July 2017.

Horrifyingly, statistics show that if a struggling person views suicide as a viable option, anything that triggers suicidal thoughts in that person can promote that belief and even advance it to the point of action.[11] Dr. Victor Schwartz at the NYU School of Medicine explained that most teens can watch shows like *13 Reasons Why* and not walk away with suicidal thoughts or behaviors, but he expressed concern for young people watching the show who have a tendency toward mental health problems or even existing undiagnosed problems.[12] These issues are known risk factors for suicide.

In a panic, many schools and parent groups issued stern warnings to teens not to watch *13 Reasons Why*. Unfortunately, these warnings only served to amplify the message of the show, and teens' attention and conversation around suicide has grown instead of lessened as a result. Even more unfortunately, adolescent behavioral health became a medical specialty only fairly recently, and not all adults will consider mental illness as a possible reason for a teen's behavioral or emotional difficulty. It's why only about a third of US adolescents with a diagnosable, treatable mental disorder ever receive treatment. Sadly, critical help often comes too late.

Suicide Awareness Efforts

In some cases, as with National Suicide Prevention Week, suicide awareness is a good thing. In others, it's a mixed bag. One that's hugely popular and seems to be a good influence is the song "1-800-273-8255" by rapper Logic with Alessia Cara and Khalid. The title of the song is the number for the National Suicide Prevention Lifeline, and the music video depicts a young African American man struggling with suicidal thoughts and extreme depression as a result of bullying, feeling ostracized, and being misunderstood because he's homosexual. The song and video give an example of how calling the Lifeline can help in moments of extreme crisis and desperation.

The #BlueWhaleChallenge also gained popularity in early 2017 and was linked to multiple deaths by suicide. The challenge, which originated in Russia, was created to encourage participants to complete increasingly harmful "dares" that involve self-harm over the course of fifty days, culminating in a final challenge to commit suicide. In July 2017, at least two American teen suicides (one broadcasted his suicide on social media) were linked to the challenge.

Perhaps the most notable occurrence of suicide references in mainstream culture is the use of "You should kill yourself" or "kill yourself" (often shortened as "kys" online) as an insult. This is careless language. It's meant as a sarcastic response when someone does something completely stupid, rather than as an actual encouragement to kill oneself. But language is crucial. It makes light of something awful, and it could reinforce the thoughts of someone who is already suicidal.

There are many pro-suicide communities online. /r/kys and /r/SanctionedSuicide are places for users to submit questions about if, when, where, and how they should commit suicide, as well as to find "death partners." One study found that the number of sites providing factual information about suicide methods had tripled between 2007 and 2014.[13]

How Seriously Should I Take Suicide Threats?

A few questions parents often wrestle with: *Don't some kids threaten suicide or self-harm just to get attention or manipulate others? Shouldn't I refuse to let my teen "manipulate" me like that?*

It's pretty important that parents fully understand the ramifications of this idea.

As previously noted, suicidal ideation and self-harm both point to an inability to express or cope with intense feelings. Most often, a young person threatens or attempts these behaviors to relieve themselves of constant, unmanageable, unbearable emotional turmoil. Some teens see self-harm or suicide as their only solution, or they do it as a way to beg for help with something they don't fully understand or have no words to describe. Sometimes they truly believe their feelings "don't matter," or they have failed at handling things on their own and feel ashamed (which makes matters worse). Philosopher and author David Foster Wallace, who struggled with lifelong depression and eventually took his own life, described his desperation this way: "The person who tries to kill herself doesn't do so because death seems suddenly appealing. The person in whom (an) invisible agony reaches a certain unendurable level will kill herself the same way a trapped person will eventually jump from the window of a burning highrise."[14]

Make no mistake about people who leap from burning windows. Their terror of falling from a great height is still just as great as it would be for you or me standing at the same window just checking out the view. The variable here is the other terror: the fire's flames. When the flames get close enough, falling to death becomes the slightly less terrible of two terrors, yet no one down on the sidewalk looking up can understand the jump. Even on the outside chance your child's motivation is to "get attention," maybe that attention is exactly what's needed.

Threats, posturing, uncontrolled anger, isolation, misbehavior, and disobedience are all symptoms in kids that should make us ask, "Why?" With the rates of teen suicide and self-harm rising, we can't afford to blow off our kids' attempts to be seen and heard, no matter how delinquent it may seem. Something serious is always behind this kind of behavior, and the real problem can be missed by parents who demand respect before giving it. We must protect our teens and limit the "exasperation" factor (Ephesians 6). First make sure they aren't in severe emotional trouble before turning on the accusations. If there's truly no emotional danger, a few minutes of active listening will confirm it—you won't spoil your child or enable poor behavior in your teen by listening to them.

We've heard people wonder why a teen who "seemed so happy" or "had so much going for them" would commit suicide. Why would apparently happy teens do this? Many teens who have suicidal thoughts or who self-harm are experts at hiding their pain. Often they can't explain it well, it doesn't make sense to them, or they believe it is wrong or dangerous to address it openly. It's crucial to see beyond what a teen projects to what's really going on.

Things to Stay Aware Of

- Behavioral health (mental illness, substance abuse, learning difficulties)
- Personality characteristics (low self-esteem, loneliness, social isolation or exclusion, low tolerance for stress, poor coping skills or body image)
- Adverse life circumstances (death of a loved one, interpersonal difficulties, disciplinary or legal problems, abuse, trauma, serious illness)
- Risky behavior (alcohol/drug use, delinquency, aggressive/violent behavior, sexual activity)
- Family circumstances (history of suicide or self-harm, familial mental illness, parental divorce or marriage difficulties, financial problems, over/under-protective or highly critical parenting style)
- Environmental factors (negative experiences at school, lack of respect or acceptance of differences, limited safety at school, weapons present on campus, limited access to mental health care, exposure to stigma or discrimination)

What Steps Can I Take to Prevent Self-Harm and Suicide?

Even with the wide variety of risk factors, powerful defensive measures exist. Studies on teen incidence of suicide and self-harm suggest ways to prevent and even heal the issues leading to suicide and self-harm in teens.

- Having a strong set of core values based on a growing faith in Christ.
- Going through intentional positive reinforcement and self-care training.
- Possessing emotional intelligence, adaptability, resilience, self-discipline, good coping and problem-solving skills.
- Possessing a sense of control, self-esteem, frustration tolerance, healthy body image.
- Getting regular exercise.
- Participating in school groups such as sports and music.
- Receiving familial and social support (parental involvement, active listening, family closeness, availability of friends and caring adults, helping with school success, modeling socially healthy behavior).
- Having access to effective health care.
- Being in a safe school community where young people feel valued, heard, and successful.
- Restricting the use of weapons, alcohol, and drugs.

How Would I Know If My Son/Daughter Is Suicidal or Self-Harming?

Any one of the following behaviors could indicate your child is at risk of suicide and needs intervention.

- Talk or interaction on social media interaction about suicide or wanting to die.

- Evidence of a suicide plan (such as an online search history, the obtaining of a weapon, or a stockpile of over-the-counter medications).
- Talk of "feeling hopeless," having "no reason to live," feeling "trapped," feeling they are "a burden" to others, or experiencing unbearable pain, fear, or trouble.
- Statements like "You won't have to worry about me for much longer" or "Soon all my troubles will be over." (They might even begin to give away some of their stuff.)
- Increasing use of drugs or alcohol, including over-the-counter medications.
- Increasingly risky, reckless behavior.
- Easily induced agitation or rage.
- Frequent sleep disturbances (too much, too little, nightmares).
- Isolation or withdrawal, especially from people or activities they used to enjoy. Increasingly rapid or extreme mood swings.

Remember, if you even suspect your child has suicidal thoughts or plans, stop reading and take action now.

The following symptoms may indicate the presence of self-harming behavior:

- Clusters of scars, cuts, scratches, or burns on the wrists, hands, or forearms (although those who self-harm may choose any place on their body)
- Frequent bruising or use of bandages
- Hair loss or bald patches on the scalp
- Isolation or withdrawal
- Wearing long sleeves, pants, or wristbands in hot weather
- Claiming frequent accidents or mishaps resulting in injury

How Can I Talk about This with My Teen?

Try one or more of these conversation openers . . .

- "Tell me more about what is happening to you. I'm here to listen."
- "How are you feeling? Have you felt like this before?"
- "I'm worried about you. It looks like you're going through a difficult time." (Then list the behaviors you've observed.)
- "I care. I want to listen and understand. What do you want me to know about the way you feel and what's going on?"
- "Can you talk to me about what you're experiencing? Do you feel like you want to?"

As we've talked about throughout the book, teens are experiencing different things than previous generations have. The book *Late Bloomers* exposes this: "The rise (in depression) seems to have much more to do with the way young people experience the world."[15] Teens might choose to run from underlying anxiety and depression with a myriad of behaviors and distractions ranging from video games, escapism, cutting, social media, overworking in school or sports, or just plain busyness. Help them engage in conversation about it. Seek help if you believe it is needed, but don't forget to start a conversation about it. Remind your teen that you see them, you love them, and God loves them.

14

Drugs

Having kids is terrifying because parenting is like walking around with your heart outside your chest.

Meg Meeker, MD[1]

Relationships are the engine of God's transformative work in us. And it is often when those relationships are most difficult, when the differences between us are most profound, that the deepest of God's sanctifying, reconciling work is done.

David Kinnaman and Gabe Lyons[2]

Teens don't change because of correction or the display of authority; they change because of a relationship.

Mark Gregston[3]

Despite being in the middle of a challenging college semester, a young man decided to build a deck at 1 a.m. Why? Because he was taking the stimulant known as speed on a regular basis so he could handle his class load. He would push hard studying for an upcoming test and stay awake for days, then crash hard and disappear for a while, presumably to catch up on sleep. The mindset and values that drove this man to use an illegal drug are the same as those that drive the abuse of prescription ones like Adderall and Ritalin.

Drugs are confusing. They are constantly being reevaluated by the FDA for whether they are useful, legal, harmful, helpful, or have a ridiculously long list of side effects (that are usually terrifying). Drugs have always been a big deal but are becoming more confusing by the year. Drugs need to be part of your ongoing conversation with your kids.

Adderall and Ritalin are legal and less addictive than street stimulants and are helpful for treating various conditions, most notably Attention Deficit Hyperactivity Disorder, or ADHD. But they, too, are widely abused and misused.

Stimulants, Like Adderall

There is a lot of confusion and shame surrounding the use of prescription stimulants. *How should parents of kids with ADHD approach their treatment? How does the cultural mindset that says stimulants are necessary for succeeding at life, regardless of whether one has ADHD, impact all of us and drive the market for stimulants? And how do we combat the mentality that success is worth going to any length to achieve?*

Stimulants act on the central nervous system to speed up the normal activities of the brain, effectively making people feel more energetic and alert (as opposed to depressants, like alcohol, which slow down the normal activities of the brain). Cocaine and methamphetamine (meth) are street drugs that fall within the stimulant category. The two most well-known prescribed Schedule II stimulants (typically prescribed for the treatment of ADHD and narcolepsy) are Adderall and Ritalin, which are two different types of stimulants. Adderall is amphetamine (other brand names are

Dexedrine and Vyvanse), whereas Ritalin is methylphenidate (other brand names are Concerta, Methylin, and Daytrana).

How are these different from meth? Meth, molly, and ecstasy are all Schedule I illicit drugs with amphetamine as part of their chemical composition. (In fact, because meth is chemically related to less potent amphetamines, people often refer to meth as an amphetamine.)

Methamphetamine and amphetamine are actually similar. Meth is more powerful and addictive, but both do the following:

Increase blood pressure and heart rate

Speed up metabolism

Raise body temperature

Increase energy

Cause feelings of euphoria

Increase focus

Create a desire to be active and productive

Although most people take prescription medications responsibly, an estimated 54 million people (more than 20 percent of those aged twelve and older) have used such medications for nonmedical reasons at least once in their lifetime.

Obviously, any drug is dangerous because it has the potential to be abused, and prescription stimulants are no different. They're dangerous if people take them in ways other than how they were prescribed for many reasons, including but not limited to the following:

- The risk of addiction due to the associated euphoria
- Increased risk of side effects (they increase heart rate and blood pressure)
- Lack of knowledge about side effects
- Possibility of overdose

- Not being monitored by a medical professional who can mitigate the drug's negative effects on the body

Something that's encouraging is that research hasn't found a link between children with ADHD who take medication and substance abuse later in life. However, there does seem to be a link between people who abuse stimulants and other types of substance abuse.

Where's All This Pressure Coming From?

What's underneath these drugs? Pressure. We live in a pressurized culture. As adults, the easiest response to friends and co-workers to the dreaded question, "How are you doing?" seems to be "stressed." Is stressed the new busy? If we adults are feeling this much stress and anxiety, how much more are the teenagers around us feeling? A lot. And it's coming from different directions.

Pressure from parents and doctors: As we already mentioned, one of the values that drives prescription stimulant abuse is the pressure to achieve. In an article about New York teens, a coordinator at an outpatient rehab facility says she's met many parents who are quick to prescribe medication for their kids. These parents are often reliant on substances themselves. Another problem is that some doctors are too quick to prescribe medication. Some students even feel the fear of doctors overprescribing drugs.

Teens are pressured to take stimulants for various reasons. One New York doctor said he sees it as his duty to prescribe Adderall to children in low-income families because the families can't afford to get their kids any other kind of help to succeed academically.[4] Talk about propping up the American Dream! Some parents admit to giving it to their kids to improve their grades or energy levels. Obviously, this is a huge concern because children are still developing, the drugs are addictive, and the parents are teaching their kids to rely on medication instead of learning emotional maturity, healthy coping mechanisms, how to set boundaries, and how to say no.

People also tend to believe that if a doctor prescribes a medication, then it's "safe," which might not be true at all. Plenty of highly addictive, dangerous drugs (morphine, for example) are used legally for medical reasons.

Peer and academic pressure: High school and college students feel the deep pressure to perform in academics, relationships, and sports. While peer pressure is a timeless "always conversation," drugs as an easy escape are a timely "now conversation."

We talked to a college student who recently transferred universities and overheard some students talking about how they were interested in trying Adderall so they could study more effectively. Another man described the highly competitive, cutthroat environment he encountered in law school. Every year, the school cut the students who were in the bottom 10 percent of the class. For fear of that, he took Adderall every day and studied for a dozen hours straight to remain in the top 1 percent of the class. He eventually burned out and dropped out without finishing his degree. Many adults use prescription stimulants to increase their output at work. There is a real danger that students who abuse stimulants to make it through college or grad school will carry that habit into their careers.

Unfortunately, prescription drugs of all sorts have come into the limelight via Hollywood and celebrities in the last decade or so. The 2011 film *Limitless* was based on the idea that a drug could unlock the entire human mind and make one, well, limitless. In addition, though some athletes take stimulants as prescribed for treatment of real medical conditions (Olympic gold medalist Simone Biles being one), and some, like former NFL player Eben Britton, have been clear that they started down the road of Adderall use in order to keep up with the physical and mental demands of their sport. In addition, some of today's most popular songs and artists normalize the use of "addys."

A recent search for "addy" on lyrics.com yielded 81 lyrics, many referring to Adderall. Many of the songs are from well-known hip-hop artists like Nicki Minaj ("Miami"), Future ("Patek Water,"

"Neva Missa Lost," "Sorry"), Travis Scott ("90210"), 21 Savage ("Mad Stalkers"), and Lil Wayne & Big Sean ("Beware"). However, the biggest influence on the culture surrounding Adderall abuse may be "emo" rap. This sub-genre gets its nickname because the artists, like the emo punks before them, feel bad. But unlike their predecessors, who analyzed their feelings with painstaking detail, these rappers don't really care to analyze themselves; they feel bad, they don't know why, so they'll take drugs to fix it. Some of the well-known artists at the forefront of this sub-genre are deceased rapper XXX-Tentacion (who unabashedly rapped about Adderall and Xanax, or "xannys," in many of his songs); Lil Peep (who died of a reported overdose at the age of 21 and was open about his prescription drug use); Lil Xan (short for Xanax); Lil Uzi Vert; Yung Lean; and $uicide Boy$. But it's not just rap culture. Justin Bieber has been open about his (legal) Adderall use (it was prescribed for his ADHD), and Jessica Simpson was reportedly abusing it to lose weight at one point.

Obviously, it's impossible to list every celebrity who uses prescription drugs (or sings about them), but it offers some insight as to why their use is on the rise. All of these people are experiencing immense pressure to "be the best" in their sphere. Enough pressure built up for them to do whatever it takes—including drugs. It speaks loudly about what our society values. And if the ones who actually are the best are feeling that pressure, then we can be sure that those who are just getting started (playing high school sports, being in high school band, singing at open mics, putting their first vlogs on YouTube, posting their photography on Instagram) are feeling that pressure too. Are we teaching teens that becoming the best is worth doing anything to get there? We sure hope not.

Marijuana, Weed, Ganja, Grass, Hash, Reefer—Whatever You Want to Call It

More states are legalizing marijuana for medical and recreational use. People from all walks of life are using it, not just the

Cheeto-binging twenty-four-year-old playing video games in mom's basement stereotype. Currently, marijuana is the most widely used illicit drug in the United States among both teens and adults. Given the widespread popularity of the drug, it's something we should be talking about with our kids. Although we all know of it, it's important to be thoughtful in how we decide what to think about it. So rather than allowing our kids' friends and pop culture to disciple our teens, let's initiate the conversation and allow them to ask questions. That way, we can disciple them into a deeper understanding of God's best for their lives and for the world he created.

Fifty-two percent of Americans say they have used marijuana at some point during their lives. About 55 million adults say they have used it one or two times within the past year. Forty-five percent of high school seniors say they have used it, and about 6 percent use it every day.[5] According to a recent survey, teen marijuana use is holding steady at its current rate.[6] These findings contrast with teen cigarette and opioid use, which are both declining (although we should note that vaping/juuling is increasingly popular). Because marijuana is becoming more normalized, it is very probable its use will grow over time. A recent survey found that 61 percent of Americans are in favor of legalizing marijuana.[7]

Marijuana affects people in a variety of ways. It impacts the user's judgment and motor skills. It also increases the heart rate, so it's possible that using it has more severe effects on people with heart disease. Some research implies that there is a relationship between early pot use and the subsequent development of schizophrenia, but the evidence is inconclusive on this point. When people smoke marijuana, it takes only minutes for the drug to make its way into the bloodstream and then the brain, giving them a high. While the high passes fairly quickly, THC can remain in the body for days following use, and "about 30 percent of ingested THC (and its metabolites) may remain in the body a full week after smoking and may continue to affect mental and physical functions subtly."[8] In fact, the remnants from a single large dose of THC may be detectable up to three weeks later.[9]

Let's Talk about Opioids

While it's not unusual for the entertainment industry to glorify drug use, it's also not uncommon to read about celebrities dying from drug overdoses. One of the most famous of these cases was when actor Heath Ledger died in 2008 from overdosing on prescription medication. You might also recall actor Philip Seymour Hoffman's passing in 2014, as well as Prince's in 2016. More recently, 21-year-old rapper Lil Peep died. What did all of these deaths have in common? Opioids were either the cause or were a contributing factor. Between 1999 and 2015, the number of prescription opioid abuses that have led to death have more than quadrupled.[10]

Authors of *Buzzed: The Straight Facts About the Most Used and Abused Drugs from Alcohol to Ecstasy* define *opiates* as "any drugs, natural or synthetic, that produce the characteristic opiate effects: the combination of a dreamy, euphoric state, lessened sensation of pain, slowed breathing, constipation, and pinpoint pupils."[11] The term *opioid*, which we will be using, is a slightly more generic word referring to substances that cause these effects.

Happily, teen opioid use has been declining lately, compared with the use of marijuana (which is holding steady) and vaping (which is on the rise). What's troubling, however, is that even though opioid use among teenagers is falling, teen deaths from opioid overdoses are increasing. In fact, opioid deaths have increased so alarmingly that in February 2018, US Attorney General Jeff Sessions announced a new task force that will target makers and distributors of prescription painkillers "who have contributed to an epidemic of fatal overdoses by selling too much of the addictive drugs."[12]

It's not uncommon for teenagers to abuse prescription painkillers and to mix them with other substances, such as alcohol, marijuana, cocaine, or amphetamines. Prescription (and over-the-counter) drugs are the third most widely abused substances among teens in the United States who are fourteen years old and older, with alcohol and marijuana being the first and second.[13] In addition to stimulants and depressants, teenagers often abuse prescription drugs of all kinds. Got pain? You can kill it, or at least numb it for a while.

Final Thoughts

It's a scary world, and the thought of your teen abusing drugs is a big deal. Yes, it can lead to all kinds of dangers, but we want to push you back to two things we've talked about throughout the book: putting on your "I'm not shocked" face and investing in conversation.

If you find out your teen has been taking drugs or is around kids who are, breathe deeply and try not to look shocked. Engage in conversation about why they wanted to or felt like they needed to take drugs. Calm yourself down and try to focus on your relationship. Don't take it personally and don't go straight to the reminder that "someday you're going to have to list this on a job application." Breathe. Pray. And reenter the conversation with your kid about what is behind the drug use. Many times parents look back to the conversation about their teen's drug use as a turning point of trust in their relationship.

SECTION 4

WHAT NOW?

15

You Can Do It!

When I was a boy of 14, my father was so ignorant I could hardly stand to have the old man around. But when I got to be 21, I was astonished at how much the old man had learned in 7 years.

Samuel Clemens, aka Mark Twain

There is no safe investment. To love at all is to be vulnerable. Love anything, and your heart will certainly be wrung and possibly broken.

C. S. Lewis, *The Four Loves*

The thief's purpose is to steal, kill and destroy. My purpose is to give life in all its fullness.

Jesus[1]

You are jolted from your sleep with loud music and clanging around in the bathroom. Your teen is getting ready for school. So you crawl out of bed before the alarm rings, determined to make the best of it. You set out on a mission to get yourself ready, throw some food together, gather up what you need for the day, and give the dreaded ten-minute warning to your kids to get in the car. You're helping all the kids get ready, but one of them can't find a sock and another one needs to have a form signed.

Your teen is cranky on the way to school. When you're about to pull into the crowded school drop-off line, they ask you if you can pick them up early, and you remind them you have a job (which is also why you have a home to live in) and a crucial meeting you can't move. They get out of the car with disgust, not even giving you a look. You head to work frazzled and feeling like a terrible parent. The residue from the morning seems to stick to you all day. You're frustrated by their sense of entitlement and endless expectations of you.

Somehow, every human in your family makes their way back home that night. They want food, and they want it now. You scramble to throw together a dinner more than half of the family will refuse to eat. Dinner is an underwhelming struggle and collision of bad attitudes. Again.

Homework is frustrating your teen, but they don't want your help. The other kids are fighting, and you've had it with the negativity and teenage moods and attitude.

As you're ready to collapse into bed, you walk past your teen's room to see them tearing up. Your first thought: *Oh no! What is wrong?* Your second thought is, *This always happens right when I'm ready to crawl into bed!* You sit down on their bed and engage the conversation. You realize they are wrestling through anxiety, struggling to keep up in science class, likely to get cut from the soccer team, and being made fun of at school. All this is unfolding while they are trying to process the negativity in their social media feeds. They end the day crying on your bed for an hour. You're exhausted from the long day, and you're counting the hours before you have to wake up and do it all again tomorrow. You remember your interactions on the ride to school and during the dinner struggle, and you feel guilty.

There's more to every teen emotion, attitude, or story than what pokes above the surface. You care about your teen. When they struggle, you struggle. When they hurt, you hurt. Family life can be chaotic for all of us. In the best-case scenario, parenting is hard. So is navigating the journey of the teen years. Both sides are riddled with doubt and insecurity. No one who has half a heart can call parenting teens an easy road. We feel for you. We pray for you, but we also want to help.

Why You?

For its first five years, Axis spoke directly to teens only. We were connecting. They were engaged. Teachers, chaplains, and student pastors gave us great feedback. We wanted to "be the best interactive presentation kids had ever seen," and many days we accomplished that. Some even described our team as "catalytic." But something was off. They didn't know what to do next, even after a multiday speaking event we were part of. So we went back to the drawing board.

We came back to our convictions that you, their parents, are the long-term solution for your kids—not us. And we started viewing ourselves as a research assistant for you. We started creating content for you. Although our *what* hasn't changed (cultivating lifelong faith), our *who* simply had to. We didn't abandon our initial strategy; we strengthened it. We are still sending out teams to speak at schools, churches, and conferences across the country. Our speakers are awesome young adults who are relevant to teens and passionate about helping them discover and live a lifelong faith. We still exist for the next generation, but we do that through *you*. We want to encourage *you*. We want to empower *you*. We love your kids, and we know that if we can help you, we can help your kids.

We're trying to help you point your kids in the right direction through thousands of micro conversations. We love the words of

Proverbs 22:6 (MESSAGE): "Point your kids in the right direction—when they're old they won't be lost." You are God's plan for your kids. There's a generational passing of the faith. That's how God planned it.

This whole parenting journey is insecure, even on the best days. It's interesting to us because there's this "command with a promise" for children to obey and honor your parents that you will gain long life (Ephesians 6:3). But there's no promise in reverse. Wouldn't it be great if there was a verse that said, "Parents, disciple your kids and they are guaranteed be wise and experience a fruitful life"? If you're reading this, we bet you want to give your kids the best chance possible for a thriving lifelong faith in Jesus. And for whatever reason, some of that is in your control, and a lot of it isn't.

Before you close this book, we want to encourage you. Satan comes to steal, kill, destroy, discourage, distract, disenchant, and practice many other forms of death (John 10:10). His evil plan is to make you think passing on lifelong faith and influencing your kid toward Jesus is impossible and just plain not worth it. But Jesus brings full and overflowing life. Jesus breathes dreams into nightmares. Jesus repairs relationships and seasons that have been ripped apart.

One father recalls the nightmare of a season when his son's depression spun into suicidal thoughts. No parent wants to imagine the moment when their child is struggling to find a reason to live. Now the father says the struggle of that season was the turning point bringing them closer. Through pain, struggle, intentionality, and conversation, God turned that nightmare into a more connected relationship.

We've worked the spectrum of the why, how, and what of conversation with your teen. Chances are you have one or more areas where you say, "I just don't know if I have it in me. I don't know if I have the tools." We don't make a habit of yelling at Axis, but I (David) have been known to yell at parents. With all my might I yell in your direction (imagine a locker-room scene in a movie): "*You have what it takes! You can do this!*" I know you doubt that. I know you feel anger, fatigue, frustration, and the shame that accompanies those feelings. That means you love your teen.

You may try to resist it, but you're still the biggest influence on your child's life. Period. For good or for ill, they're going to act like you, love like you, talk like you. It's sociologically true, theologically true, and experientially true. So, picture our team reading this Scripture over you as a kind of commissioning.

> "O my people, listen to my instructions.
>> Open your ears to what I am saying,
>> for I will speak to you in a parable.
> I will teach you hidden lessons from our past—
>> stories we have heard and known,
>> stories our ancestors handed down to us.
> We will not hide these truths from our children;
>> we will tell the next generation
>> about the glorious deeds of the Lord,
>> about his power and his mighty wonders.
> For he issued his laws to Jacob;
>> he gave his instructions to Israel.
> He commanded our ancestors
>> to teach them to their children,
>> so the next generation might know them—
>> even the children not yet born—
>> and they in turn will teach their own children.
> So each generation should set its hope anew on God,
>> not forgetting his glorious miracles
>> and obeying his commands.
> Then they will not be like their ancestors—
>> stubborn, rebellious, and unfaithful,
>> refusing to give their hearts to God."
>
> Psalm 78:1–8 NLT

At the beginning of the book we started with a few stories. We talked about Jesus' call to disciple your kids. We peeled open our life stories and how they birthed a ministry. We took you into the crowd where Steve Jobs introduced a revolutionary phone that changed culture forever. We helped you know what posture to take with your teen. We reminded you to practice your "I'm not shocked" face in the mirror. And we talked about things you should know so you can begin and continue crucial conversations. Now we'll come back to where this all started, the story of Jesus and his plan for the spread of the Gospel.

Jesus' Final Lecture

After Jesus was raised from the dead, he spent forty days teaching the disciples one last class. This last class led to Jesus' last words before ascending to heaven: "You will receive power when the Holy Spirit comes upon you. And you will be my witnesses, telling people about me everywhere—in Jerusalem, throughout Judea, in Samaria, and to the ends of the earth" (Acts 1:8 NLT).

Remember, we believe parents are the most effective missionaries. God designed this plan. If you're a parent, you're a missionary. The fear is real. The cultural gap is real. But so is the power and presence of God in your life and family. We are hearing stories of parents all over the world having one ongoing conversation en route to lifelong faith for their children.

When we started Axis, we were two guys with a huge heart for the next generation, but we were stuck between generations. As our kids and our convictions grew, we shifted the focus of the ministry to the parents. This is the evolution of our ministry.

Here are my (Jeremiah's) desires for my kids.

I want them to love Jesus like I love Jesus, or better. At first Axis was a response to friends and fringe family members leaving the faith. I definitely don't want my kids to leave the faith. I want them to thrive. I'm trusting these promises from Scripture. I'm leaning on Deuteronomy 6 to teach God to them as we go along the way. I'm trusting Proverbs 22:6 for them to have wisdom in their old age because of this foundation. I want to hear Psalm 78 traces in their lives where they "tell the coming generation the glorious deeds of the Lord." I want to know that if you put in the focused effort to raise up the next generation, God will reward it as much as he sees fit.

Here are my (David's) desires for my kids.

I want them to be contributing to the world. I want their faith to not just be something that they think or something that they check off, but actually something that informs their creating value in the universe—not where I'm making it happen for them, but just where I get to encourage them and form them and make connections with them. I want to be in relationship with them where we're doing things together and I get to be active in their life.

I want them to be a great wife or great husband. I want them to be secure in their masculinity or femininity, their identity, their gender. I don't want them to be confused about who they are. When it comes to their faith, I want them to have a big-picture understanding for God.

I want to be in a relationship with them, on their terms, in cool ways. I want to continue sharing wisdom with them and having them share their wonder with me. I want to see them thriving in marriage, connected to a church, and loving their family well. I want to connect them to a fulfilling future.

From Caring Adults to Influencers

The word *influencer* has stormed onto the scene in the last few years. An influencer is common vernacular today for someone with a presence online (mainly on social media and YouTube). They generally have a whole lot of followers. Your teens look up to them. Technically, we're all influencers in one way or another, but the term is used specifically to refer to a person who uses their social media presence and platforms to influence others to believe, buy, or do something (or commonly, all three).

An influencer ultimately uses his or her power to market products (their own or someone else's) to their large online following, and by doing so, they also make money, which is why it's now considered a job. Many influencers start out on Instagram or You-Tube with a small audience and build it by posting consistently and making connections with their followers. Typically, they make a name for themselves inside a niche and become an authority in that niche.

Influencers are everywhere. Some of them are famous for being famous (think Paris Hilton or the Kardashians). Some of them have an incredible skill and have built a large following (subscribers or followers) around themselves. Some of them play video games while giving commentary (hard to believe that's a thing). Some of them are paid for advertising brands and products. All of them are shaping culture, especially youth culture. Their names (or fake influencer names) are widely recognized by teens around the world.

Influencer Marketing Hub reports, "70% of teens think that YouTubers are more reliable than celebrities and 88% of consumers trust online recommendations as much as face-to-face recommendations. Social media influencers are real people, and they're more likely to be authentic and to interact with their audience, so brands are starting to take note."[2]

Even with massive followings, these influencers don't have the kind of influence on your teen that you do. We started the book by thanking you for caring for your teen. The first tool in your toolbelt is your care for them. You love them and you want them to thrive. But you are much more than just a caring adult; you are an influencer. Because you care for them, you have influence with them. It may not seem like it. They might not seem open to your input, but you have influence.

Other influencers will come and go in your teen's life, but you have a sixty-year conversation ahead of you. You get to play the long game. You will watch them grow in and out of phases, struggle, succeed, fail, wander, win, lose, react, cry, and process it all with you along the way. *You* are the influencer.

You Are Heroes

We love hearing stories of influencers shaping their kids. You are our heroes. Your one lifelong conversation starts as whispers over a crib and morphs into texts to your kid at college and visits to see the grandkids. Someday you will find yourself in a love stupor for your grandkids.

It's so thrilling to hear these parenting stories. One mom and dad told their teen, "You can tell me anything," and along the way their kids told them anything and everything. It made them mad, broke their hearts, but it planted seeds for many beautiful things to sprout. Another set of parents practiced the "I'm not shocked" face, because they let their eighteen-year-old eventually have full access to his phone, and they knew he was probably going to look at porn sometime. But they also knew that he had to work through that on his own. We have even seen love in the parents who yell at their kids because they love them so much, and they don't know how to do anything else, and they apologize. We love hearing about the kids who are good at asking for forgiveness because their parents do it enough to each other and to them. We love hearing about parents who find every excuse to take their daughters out on breakfast dates and do another activity to connect with their son.

Parenting Is Hard

Parents often tell us, "It's harder than I thought it would be." Everyone has suggestions for parents until you become one. You get caught up in the rhythm and the flow, and you come home, and you're tired, and they're hungry. At times you might feel help-less. At other times you'll feel misunderstood. That's part of the parenting journey. It's hard. It has an edge. It surprises you every day. It's not a cake walk.

There's an irony in parenting no one ever told us: We are wres-tling with the same insecurities our kids wrestle with. We wrestle through insecurities while others, our teens included, are watch-ing. It's hard being an imperfect parent on display. We've been given the charge to raise adults, not to raise children. You need to have fun, but you need to have serious conversations along the way.

Parenting Is Confusing

Teens' parents have to learn to deal with ambiguity. It's confusing because there's always going to be something new. There's always going to be something we're bad at. Or something we don't know about that we're silenced on. There's always new territory to pio-neer, because it's a soul that you've birthed or adopted, not just a growing body. Parenting is never something you just figure out or have the market cornered on. And parents of teens have to learn to be okay with that. The same ambiguity that drives you crazy will drive you to reliance on Almighty God.

Parenting Is Good

God created parenting, and it's good. Don't be in a hurry. You don't have to be right all the time. Third-way parents have a growth mindset—they're always learning. Get your head out of your phone and pay attention to your kids. Have some fun along the way with them. They will help you grow and mature, and they will push you. There will be conversations you think will be awful, and twenty minutes later your hearts feel connected, and they say, "I love you."

Parenting Is a Puzzle

Parenting is this giant jigsaw that you get to figure out patiently. It won't come together all at once when you've read this book (although that would be awesome). It comes a moment at a time, a decision at a time, and a conversation at a time. There are plenty of things you won't understand about your teen, but sometimes it will just click. Keep searching for the corner pieces, those turning points where the rest of the parenting puzzle starts to make sense.

Parenting Is a Team Sport

Don't do parenting alone. We want you to be in community, because you're better in community than you are in isolation. Find other parents who care about discipling their kids, and don't give your best to the parents just trying to "survive these awful teenage years." Find a church that can support you in the calling to disciple your kids. Utilize our team like a supportive research assistant, your own personal culture translator. Parenting teens—it's takes a team, y'all.

Parenting Is Delayed Gratification

I (David) will never forget an analogy from my grandfather. He was a man's man and worked in the lumberyard business. When he reflected on his grandpa (my great-great-grandfather), he thought of the rings of a tree. We have clocks and Apple watches and calendars that show hours and days that pass, but trees tell time too. So do kids. Parenting doesn't tell time in hours and days; it tells time in seasons, years, and decades. It takes patience and a long view. Someday maybe my great-great-grandson will talk about me, or maybe he will just pass on the legacy of faith in our family.

Parents, we are playing the long game, one that won't give you the return on your investments now. We want the best for our kids, and if you do the work now, you'll see bigger rewards later. Of course you want to see results in your kids, but don't be dependent on seeing those results right now.

When you disciple your child, it will feel slow. Sometimes you'll even feel like you're moving backward. James K. A. Smith gives this helpful reminder to parents: "Effective Christian formation of young people might look like failure for a time."[3] Researchers estimate it costs a quarter of a million dollars to raise a child. It's a slow investment, but it can have eternal returns. You think it's great to be a dad when you have a newborn. Then you have a two-year-old, a five-year-old, a thirty-six-year-old, and it just keeps getting better. Just talk to smitten grandparents.

Yes, There Is Hope

"You don't even understand how big of a deal Axis is for me." When I (Jeremiah) heard this, my heart nearly exploded in my chest. This mom deeply loves her kids and has been looking for something better than googling "How to disciple my kid." She finally found it. Axis can actually help her! We hope the phrase *third-way parenting* gives you hope just reading it. Yes, it's possible not to live in crippling fear or look the other way in disengagement. It's possible to not just survive parenting through the teen years, but to build a foundation there for the rest of your children's lives.

We remember the mom who finally realized that meaningful interaction with her teen was possible. After engaging with our parent guides, she said, "We've just started the conversation with our kid on social media, and I can't believe how many conversations we have had." We love hearing stories of the first step, and we get to hear them often. Our end goal is not speaking to your kids; it's you starting and continuing your lifelong conversation with them. After journeying through the book, hopefully you have inspiration and next steps for the conversation. Don't get distracted, start them now.

And here's something you might not know: Those conversations with your kids are strengthening your faith too. They are helping you just as much as they're helping your kid. A pastor recently told our team, "It's cool that you guys are telling me that you want to help our teenagers, but really what I care about as a parent is the spiritual growth of my parishioners. And I believe that you guys are a path for making my adults more healthy and helping them understand their faith better than they ever have."

This was a good reminder. Yes, it's about the next generation of the faith who will be raising their kids in twenty years, but it's also about you growing right now. That's the secret mission of Axis: to make you a better follower of Jesus and me a better follower of Jesus by forcing us to be teachers of our kids and entering that uncomfortable space of leading and discipling.

We aren't the hero in your kid's story—you are. It starts by stepping into your teen's world. Then you can bring empathy for your child and their world. You'll start connecting with the heart of your teen. It's not about connecting with an app, a band, or an idea—it's about connecting with their heart. When you're confident stepping into your teen's world, fear won't have a stranglehold on you. Connection yields confidence, and that confidence yields more connection.

So be confident! This is your conversation to start, to continue, and to have every day for the rest of your life. And that confidence will help you push through the fear you have about your teens.

You can be sure of a few things:

God wants you to disciple your kid.

Conversation is the way to their heart.

Instead of fighting culture or disengaging, you can engage culture.

You have what it takes to start and continue a lifelong conversation.

God is with you on this journey.

Axis is here to help!

We believe in your God-given role. It's literally why we exist. We've created resources on subjects ranging from YouTube to the Resurrection to body image to the Enneagram, and we will continue to develop resources for you as new topics arise. We send a weekly email called the *Culture Translator* that's designed to help you navigate the gaps. Our team is constantly designing new content to help you take the next step and have your next conversation with your teen. We love hearing about your breakthroughs and next steps with your teen.

Enjoy the Parenting Journey

What if you could enjoy the parenting journey? White-knuckling your way through it isn't fun. It's going to require discernment and a lot of prayer. Teens need to start making decisions for themselves. We can promise you they won't make every decision the way you would. Ask God to release you from any parental shame and guilt and start enjoying them. Parenting isn't a sprint to get your kids to the finish line. After extensive research, journalist and entrepreneur Rich Karlgaard concluded, "Early maturity—or early blooming—in no way correlated to maturity and wisdom as an older adult. Wisdom, it turns out, isn't bequeathed. It's earned."[4]

So many parents feel like they're behind the curve. Go ahead and get started. As you do, here are some challenging words from one of our favorite teen champions and grandpas, Mark Gregston.

Don't wait. Your teens need you now.

Time passes way too quickly not to take advantage of that present that is today.

Don't wait until you're no longer busy; that will never happen.

Don't wait until that special occasion; it is happening around you every day.

Don't wait until you can afford it; you can't afford not to.

Don't wait until you can find the time; it passes too quickly.

Don't miss opportunities during your teen's years; it will be gone too soon.

You will never be appreciated more or have a greater impact at any other time than the special occasion that is before you today.[5]

With the wisdom of Solomon, the words of Jesus, and the presence of the Holy Spirit, you're equipped to navigate complicated issues and connect to the heart of the teen you love. God knew your teen before you did. Ask him to reveal the real issue going on behind the behavior, the attitude, and the decisions. Don't give in to fear that causes you to fight or take flight. Engage in relationship with your child. Our team and others can give you good information, but you have to start the conversation.

Unlike when we started Axis, Jeremiah and I now both have kids. We tuck them in, monitor what they watch, and pray like crazy for them. We are starting and continuing our lifelong conversations. Even on the discouraging days, we know we'll be the biggest influence in their lives. One moment they may nominate us for parent of the year, and the next they'll make a vow never to be like us. But there is a God-designed force that brings them back to us longing for connection.

Like the pastor who only had one sermon and the loving father who only had one conversation with his daughter, life is best measured one by one. One moment, one meal, one car ride, and one influencer can change a life.

So breathe deep and lean in; you have one conversation to join.

Recommended Resources

On discipling your kids

A Parent's Guide to Discipling Teenagers by Axis

On faith and the next generation

Sticky Faith by Dr. Kara E. Powell and Dr. Chap Clark
Households of Faith by Barna Research Group

On conversation

Spiritual Conversations in the Digital Age by Barna Research Group

On youth ministry

The State of Youth Ministry by Barna Research Group

On screens and video games

Smartphone Sanity by Axis

The Tech-Wise Family by Andy Crouch
A Parent's Guide to Video Games by Axis
A Parent's Guide to Discord by Axis
A Parent's Guide to Fortnite by Axis
A Parent's Guide to League of Legends by Axis
A Parent's Guide to Minecraft by Axis
A Parent's Guide to Twitch.tv by Axis

On depression and suicide

A Parent's Guide to Depression & Anxiety by Axis
A Parent's Guide to Suicide & Self-Harm Prevention by Axis

On sexuality

Passport to Purity resources by FamilyLife
GOD'S DESIGN FOR SEX, a book series by Dr. Stan and
   Brenna Jones

On rites of passage

ManMaker Project by Chris Bruno
Primal Path course by Jon Tyson

On apologetics

A Parent's Guide to the Bible by Axis
A Parent's Guide to a Doubting Teen by Axis
A Parent's Guide to the Evidence for the Resurrection by Axis
"65 Questions Every Parent Must Answer" from Cross Examined. A list of tough questions and links to answers
   your teens might be looking for.

Holman's Quicksource Guide to Apologetics by Doug Powell. A good primer for answering questions listed in this book, as well as many more.

The Ten Most Common Objections to Christianity by Alex McFarland. An introductory book written for teenagers to answer some of the basic questions about God, Christianity, and Jesus.

Apologetics Study Bible for Students. A study Bible by Dr. Sean McDowell with tons of great articles addressing nearly every critical issue teenagers face today, written with skeptical teens in mind.

The One-Minute Apologist. A YouTube channel designed to equip students to share their faith and explain why they believe what they believe in the shortest amount of time possible (e.g., between classes).

Acknowledgments

Thank you, Jesus, for being our savior, life, and love. Thank you, God, for being our father and guide. You're our reason for being and for having one lifelong conversation.

Thanks and love to the following people:

To the countless anonymous people who've prayed for Axis at any point in our history. Prayer is our lifeblood.

To all those who've mentored, coached, and guided us before and during Axis' life as a ministry.

We wish we could put the names of each Axis team member who has contributed to this book on the cover. To our content writers and researchers who helped come up with some of the great information in this book, like Evan, Gary Alan, Hannah, Melanie, and Tony. To the original crew of employees at Axis who came in a few different waves and took giant leaps of faith to help us get started: Chad, Meghan, Daniel G, Melanie, Daniel D, Amanda, and Nicholas. To the rest of our current team at Axis who serve as research assistants for countless parents, grandparents, and mentors of the next generation: Amy, Brennan, Caleb, Charissa, Chris, CJ, Courtney, Dan, Dilynn, Jason, Kate, Kelli, Lexi, Madison, Reesey, Russell, Sarah, and Sharon. To all we didn't name who've given years of service to Axis during our crazy start-up years so we could build the foundation we live on today. To all who've spoken for Axis as part of our speaking teams over the years. To all Axis staff family members who've encouraged us to make less money and work longer hours at times for the mission of Axis.

To our amazing couples board of directors who first encouraged us to write this book: Dr. Bill and Lynne Brown (and Dr. Brown for following God's leading to create the model that Axis eventually copied and built upon), Mat and Kenzie Clouse, Tim and Christi Jenkins, Dan and Christin McClave, Gillis and Julie West, Randy and Sandy Wilcox. To Jeff and Jacqlyn Johns (our first couples board chair). To our amazing original board of directors who sacrificially helped us launch: Alex Burton, John Stonestreet, Lloyd Burton, Russ Northup, Eric Smith, Melissa Sievers, and Denise Snyder.

To the guy who helped us make this book exist and make it amazing and who worked with two very strong personalities to write it: Alan Briggs. Alan, you're a great leader, a good man, a wonderful listener, and a disciplined practitioner!

From David:

Thanks to my precious family. Shiloh, Zion, and Vale, I am honored to be your daddy. Lindsey, you are an incredible mom and an even better wife and companion. The unique sacrifices you make for us and for Axis are amazing.

To the team at Axis. I love working with you.

To my folks. Your ongoing prayer, friendship, and faithfulness mean the world to me.

To my church and youth group. Don't forget, Jesus loves you, and the Eatons love you!

To Jeremiah, the other cofounder. Thanks for working hard and sacrificing day in and day out for the Gospel!

To the thousands and thousands of families that have let Axis be your "research assistant" . . . know that we are completely honored and that we will always be in your corner. You have what it takes. The rising generation needs you, and we need them. Keep being "one conversation" parents!

From Jeremiah:

Thanks, Mom and Dad, for having great conversations with me as a kid and leading me to Jesus. Thanks, Randy and Kathy, for being wonderful in-laws and being another set of parents encouraging me in my walk with God as an adult.

To my amazing wife, Kim, for being another founder of Axis and for encouraging me and pushing us to embrace the mission of Axis and all the challenges that come with it. Also, for your great love, inspiring beauty, and unwavering support in helping me live out my great calling as a father.

Notes

Introduction: We Know You Care

1. Barna Group, *The State of Youth Ministry* (Ventura, CA: Barna Group, 2016), 47.

Chapter 1: You Are a Third-Way Parent

1. Barna Group, *The State of Youth Ministry* (Ventura, CA: Barna Group, 2016), 78.
2. Barna Group, *Spiritual Conversation in the Digital Age* (Ventura, CA: Barna Group, 2018), 7.
3. Steve Jobs in "Steve Jobs Introducing the iPhone at MacWorld 2007," You-Tube, December 2, 2010, https://www.youtube.com/watch?v=x7qPAY9JqE4.
4. Pinetops Foundation, *The Great Opportunity: The American Church in 2050* (Seattle, WA: Pinetops Foundation, 2018), 13.

Chapter 2: The Most Important Conversation

1. Mark Gregston, *Raising Teens in a Contrary Culture* (Apopka, FL: Certa Publishing, 2018), 57.
2. Joseph Grenny, Ron McMillan, Kerry Patterson and Al Switzler, *Crucial Conversations* (New York: McGraw-Hill, Edition 2, 2011), 22.
3. From a letter read by Eugene Peterson's son Leif at his memorial service, found in the Commemorative Preface to *A Long Obedience in the Same Direction: Discipleship in an Instant Society,* commemorative edition (Downers Grove, IL: InterVarsity Press, 2019), 2–3.
4. Alan Briggs, *Guardrails: Six Principles for a Multiplying Church* (Colorado Springs, CO: NavPress, 2016). This definition is referenced throughout the book.
5. From Wayne Cordeiro's personal Facebook page, September 2, 2011, https://www.facebook.com/pg/pastorwaynecordeiro/posts/?ref=page_internal. This is

also mentioned in his book *Leading on Empty; Refilling Your Tank and Renewing Your Passion.*

6. Gregston, *Raising Teens*, 21.

7. Gregston, *Raising Teens,* 25, 33.

Chapter 3: Your Wisdom, Their Wonder

1. David Kinnaman and Gabe Lyons, *Good Faith* (Grand Rapids, MI: Baker Publishing, 2016), 153.

2. Matthew 11:28 NIV.

3. As quoted in the Barna Group's *The State of Youth Ministry* (Ventura, CA: Barna Group, 2016).

4. Wess Stafford, *Just a Minute* (Chicago: Moody Press, 2014), 13.

5. Stafford, *Just a Minute*, 14.

6. Mark Gregston, *Raising Teens in a Contrary Culture* (Apopka, FL: Certa Publishing, 2018), 24.

7. Barna Group, "Jonathan Morrow on Building Lasting Faith in Gen Z," July 19, 2018, https://www.barna.com/gen-z-qa-with-jonathan-morrow/.

8. Rich Karlgaard, *Late Bloomers* (New York: Penguin Random House, 2019), 29.

9. Barna, *Youth Ministry*, 84.

10. Barna Group, "Pastors and Parents Differ on Youth Ministry Goals," March 22, 2017, https://www.barna.com/research/pastors-parents-differ-youth -ministry-goals/.

11. Sharon Galgay Ketcham, referenced in *The State of Youth Ministry* (Ventura, CA: Barna Group, 2016), 47.

12. Barna, "Pastors and Parents."

13. This section is written by Tony Miller, a valuable part of our Axis team with a heart for seeing discipleship develop among families.

14. Barna Group, *Households of Faith* (Ventura, CA: Barna Group, 2019), 128.

15. Barna, *Households*, 51.

16. Barna, *Households*, 16–17.

17. Barna, *Households*, 18.

18. Barna, *Households*, 16–17.

19. This content is created by our friends at Restoration Project, submitted by Chris Bruno, restorationproject.org.

Chapter 4: Conversation: The Hunger for WITH

1. Andy Crouch references Sherry Turkle's *Reclaiming Conversation* in *The Tech-Wise Family* (Grand Rapids, MI: Baker Publishing, 2017), 157.

2. Crouch, *Tech-Wise Family,* 157.

3. Barna Group, *The State of Youth Ministry* (Ventura, CA: Barna Group, 2016), 48.

4. Barna Group, *Households of Faith* (Ventura, CA: Barna Group, 2019), 11.

5. Barna, *Households*, 89.

6. Barna, *Households*, 107.

7. Barna, *Households*, 107.

Chapter 5: Translating Culture

1. Barna Group, *The State of Youth Ministry* (Ventura, CA: Barna Group, 2016), 87.
2. C.S. Lewis, *The Weight of Glory: And Other Addresses* (New York: HarperCollins, 2001), 26.
3. John F. Kavanaugh, *Following Christ in a Consumer Society* (New York: Orbis Books, 2006), 80.
4. Kavanaugh, *Following Christ*, 80.
5. E.D. Hirsch Jr., *Cultural Literacy: What Every American Needs to Know* (New York: Vintage Books, 1988), 2.
6. Brian Zahnd, *Beauty Will Save the World: Rediscovering the Allure and Mystery of Christianity* (Lake Mary, FL: Charisma House, 2012), xvi–xvii.
7. Anne Frank, *Diary of a Young Girl* (New York: Bantam, 1993), 171.

Chapter 6: Missionaries Cleverly Disguised As Parents

1. Alasdair MacIntyre, *After Virtue*, 2nd ed. (Notre Dame, IN: University of Notre Dame Press, 1984), 216.
2. James K.A. Smith, *You Are What You Love* (Grand Rapids, MI: Brazos Press, 2016), 112–113.
3. Smith, *You Are*, 113.
4. Smith, *You Are*, 127.

Chapter 7: Cultivating a Heart Connection

1. Martha Beck, "When You Feel Lonely," *Martha's Blog*, 2012, https://marthabeck.com/2012/11/when-you-feel-lonely/.
2. Jessica Bursztynsky, "Researchers Find E-Cigarettes Cause Lung Cancer in Mice in First Study Tying Vaping to Cancer," *CNBC*, October 7, 2019, https://www.cnbc.com/2019/10/07/e-cigarettes-cause-lung-cancer-in-mice-finds-first-study-tying-vaping-to-cancer.html.
3. Michael Joseph Blaha, MD, MPH, "5 Vaping Facts You Need to Know," Johns Hopkins Medicine, hopkinsmedicine.org, n.d., https://www.hopkinsmedicine.org/health/wellness-and-prevention/5-truths-you-need-to-know-about-vaping.

Chapter 9: The New Sex Talk

1. Mark Gregston, *Raising Teens in a Contrary Culture* (Apopka, FL: Certa Publishing, 2018), 79.
2. Gregston, *Raising Teens*, 12.
3. bangshowbiz.com, "Miley Cyrus Fluid with Sexuality," *Washington Post*, June 9, 2015, https://www.washingtonpost.com/entertainment/miley-cyrus-fluid-with-sexuality/2015/06/09/a7c4563a-0edb-11e5-a0fe-dccfea4653ee_story.html.
4. Leila Brillson, "Lily-Rose Depp & Harley Quinn Smith Shed Light on That Whole 'Queer' Thing," *Nylon* magazine, February 3, 2016, https://nylon.com/articles/lily-rose-depp-harley-quinn-smith-interview.

5. Meg Meeker, *Strong Fathers, Strong Daughters* (New York: Ballantine Books, 2007), 32.

6. Meeker, *Strong Fathers*, 23.

7. Meeker, *Strong Fathers*, 24.

8. David Kinnaman and Gabe Lyons, *Good Faith* (Grand Rapids, MI: Baker Publishing, 2016), 131.

9. Gregston, *Raising Teens*, 14.

10. Andy Crouch, *The Tech-Wise Family* (Grand Rapids, MI: Baker Publishing, 2017), 54.

Chapter 10: Smartphones

1. Andy Crouch, *The Tech-Wise Family* (Grand Rapids, MI: Baker Publishing, 2017), 63.

2. Mark Gregston, *Raising Teens in a Contrary Culture* (Apopka, FL: Certa Publishing, 2018), 28.

3. Sherry Turkle, *The Second Self: Computers and the Human Spirit*, twentieth anniversary edition (Cambridge, MA: MIT Press, 2005), 311.

4. Roald Dahl, *Charlie and the Chocolate Factory* (New York: Puffin Books, 1968), 139.

5. Crouch, *Tech-Wise Family*, 117.

6. Crouch, *Tech-Wise Family*, 109.

7. Thanks to Bob Lepine, cohost of *FamilyLife Today*, for those terms.

Chapter 11: Video Games

1. Much of the material in this chapter was originally published in the Axis *A Parent's Guide to Video Games* and the individual guides to Discord, Fortnite, Minecraft, Twitch.tv, and League of Legends.

2. "Wikipedia: Marcus Brigstocke," Wikimedia Foundation, last modified February 6, 2020, 14:47, https://en.wikipedia.org/wiki/Marcus_Brigstocke.

3. Barna Group, *Spiritual Conversation in the Digital Age* (Ventura, CA: Barna Group, 2018), 13.

4. American Psychological Association, *Resolution on Violent Video Games, 2015*. Retrieved from http://www.apa.org/about/policy/violent-video-games.aspx.

5. Brown v. Entertainment Merchants Association, 564 U.S. at 12–13 (2011), https://www.supremecourt.gov/opinions/10pdf/08-1448.pdf.

6. Andy Crouch's *Tech-Wise Family* is a good start on this topic.

Chapter 12: College

1. Gordon Govier, "How to Choose a College . . . and Keep Your Faith," *InterVarsity*, February 10, 2018, https://intervarsity.org/news/how-choose-college-and-keep-your-faith.

2. Research from Fuller Youth Institute, Axis, *A Parent's Guide to College Prep*, 2.

3. Axis, *A Parent's Guide to College Prep*, 2.

4. Axis, *College Prep*, 2.

5. Axis, *College Prep*, 5.
6. Axis, *College Prep*, 5.
7. Axis, *College Prep*, 5.
8. Axis, *College Prep*, 5.
9. Axis, *College Prep*, 5.
10. For more about this, check out the book *Mindset: The New Psychology of Success* by Carol S. Dweck, PhD (Ballantine, 2013).
11. Axis, *College Prep*, 6.
12. Axis, *College Prep*, 8.
13. Read our Axis resource *A Parent's Guide to Sexual Assault* for a deeper look.
14. In our Axis resource *A Parent's Guide to a Doubting Teen*, we discuss various arguments for the existence of God. These are hugely important, but we could not take the time and space to cover every argument against doubt.

Chapter 13: Depression and Anxiety

1. Rich Karlgaard, *Late Bloomers* (New York: Penguin Random House, 2019), 30.
2. John 16:33 NASB.
3. Axis, *A Parent's Guide to Depression and Anxiety*, 1.
4. Karlgaard, *Late Bloomers*, 11.
5. Mary Elizabeth Dallas, "10 Million U.S. Adults Seriously Considered Suicide Last Year," CBS News, September 15, 2016, 3:04 PM, https://www.cbsnews.com/amp/news/10-million-us-adults-seriously-considered-suicide-last-year/.
6. Kidsdata.org, "Child/Youth Death Rate, by Age and Cause," Lucille Packard Foundation for Children's Health, https://www.kidsdata.org/topic/659/childdeathrate-age-cause/table#fmt=2318&loc=1,2&tf=120&ch=1307,1309,446,1308,530,531,533,532,975,534,529. See also Randy Dotinga, "Suicide Can Strike Children As Young As 5, Study Warns," CBS News, September 19, 2016, 1:23 PM, https://www.cbsnews.com/amp/news/suicide-can-strike-children-as-young-as-5-study/.
7. Samantha Gluck, "Self Injury, Self Harm, Statistics and Facts," Healthy Place for Your Mental Health, last updated June 21, 2019, https://www.healthyplace.com/abuse/self-injury/self-injury-self-harm-statistics-and-facts.
8. National Center for Injury Prevention and Control, "Preventing Suicide," Division of Violence Prevention, last reviewed September 5, 2019, https://www.cdc.gov/violenceprevention/suicide/fastfact.html.
9. The American Academy of Child & Adolescent Psychiatry, "Suicide in Children and Teens," last updated June 2018, https://www.aacap.org/AACAP/Families_and_Youth/Facts_for_Families/FFF-Guide/Teen-Suicide-010.aspx.
10. Melissa Conrad Stöppler, MD, "Medical Definition of Non-Suicidal Self Injury (NSSI), MedicineNet, Mental Health Center, last reviewed on December 21, 2018, https://www.medicinenet.com/script/main/art.asp?articlekey=126496.
11. Axis, *Depression & Anxiety*, 4.
12. See our *A Parent's Guide to Depression & Anxiety* for more information.
13. "There Are Websites That Promote Suicide. That's Not Okay," Health & Science, *Washington Post*, April 23, 2017, https://www.washingtonpost.com/nat

ional/health-science/there-are-websites-that-promote-suicide-thats-not-okay/20
17/04/21/586901fc-2050-11e7-be2a-3a1fb24d4671_story.html.

14. As quoted in Axis, *Depression & Anxiety*, 6.

15. Karlgaard, *Late Bloomers* (New York: Penguin Random House, 2019), 31.

Chapter 14: Drugs

1. Meg Meeker, MD, *Strong Fathers, Strong Daughters* (New York: Ballantine Books, 2007), 60.

2. David Kinnaman and Gabe Lyons, *Good Faith: Being a Christian When Society Thinks You're Irrelevant and Extreme* (Grand Rapids, MI: Baker Publishing, 2016), 154.

3. Mark Gregston, *Raising Teens in a Contrary Culture* (Apopka, FL: Certa Publishing, 2018), 131.

4. Axis, *A Parent's Guide to Prescription Stimulants*, 5

5. Axis, *A Parent's Guide to Marijuana*, 4

6. Monitoring the Future via Axis, *Marijuana*, 4.

7. Pew Research Center via Axis, *Marijuana*, 4.

8. Cynthia Kuhn, PhD, Scott Swartzwelder, PhD, and Wilkie Wilson, PhD, *Buzzed: The Straight Facts About the Most Used and Abused Drugs from Alcohol to Ecstasy*, revised ed. (New York: W.W. Norton, 2003), 140.

9. Axis, *Marijuana*, 4.

10. The Centers for Disease Control and Prevention via Axis, *A Parent's Guide to Teens & Opioids*, 3.

11. Kuhn, et al, *Buzzed*, 177.

12. Axis, *Teens & Opioids*, 3.

13. Axis, *Teens & Opioids*, 4

Chapter 15: You Can Do It!

1. John 10:10 TLB.

2. Axis, *A Parent's Guide to Influencers*, 2.

3. James K.A. Smith, *You Are What You Love* (Grand Rapids, MI: Brazos Press, 2016), 146.

4. Rich Karlgaard, *Late Bloomers* (New York: Penguin Random House, 2019), 127.

5. Mark Gregston, *Raising Teens in a Contrary Culture* (Apopka, FL: Certa Publishing, 2018), 143.

David Eaton is the president of Axis, which he cofounded with Jeremiah Callihan in 2007. David has spoken with more than 100,000 students and parents, and now spends his time finding new ways for Axis to reach more families.

David has led partnerships between Axis and Family Life Today, MOPS, Young Life, Youth for Christ, Focus on the Family, Ravi Zacharias International Ministries, the Association of Christian Schools International, Compassion International, Word of Life, Moody Radio, The Colson Center, Care-Net, and many, many others.

David is married to his intelligent and creative wife, Lindsey, and they have three kids: Shiloh Abigail, Zion Daniel, and Vale Calvary. The Eatons live in Colorado.

Jeremiah Callihan is the CEO and cofounder of Axis, leading the vision, strategy, product development, and execution of the plan to reach as many families as possible with the Gospel. It's Jeremiah's passion to equip caring adults to be the best possible missionaries and spiritual guides to the next generation. Seeing lifetime conversations between parents and their kids that lead to lifelong faith in Jesus is what motivates Jeremiah every day.

Jeremiah lives in Colorado and has been married for fifteen years to his best friend, Kim. They're in the midst of one conversation with each of their four amazing kids. When he isn't playing catch or board games or on the trampoline with his kids, Jeremiah might be eating French toast, playing basketball, watching football, or reading a great book somewhere outside, with inspirational music in the background.

The Axis team is currently made up of twenty-seven staff members who love God and love the rising generation. We are researchers, speakers, and content creators, but most important, we are in your corner. We are your culture translation assistants. You can find us at axis.org. Let us know if you have any questions or if we need to add anything to the next edition of this book!

Alan Briggs loves bringing life-changing messages into the world through books, ebooks, and articles. He founded Stay Forth Designs to help leaders, teams, and organizations GET HEALTHY + REACH MORE IMPACT. Beyond writing, coaching, and consulting, Alan designs ridiculously refreshing experiences for leaders to recharge and collaborate. He has an amazing wife, four kids, and a dog the size of a calzone.

Others you should know about

Restoration Project is an amazing ministry for men to fully engage as fathers, husbands, and brothers. They have an awesome rite-of-passage program for fathers and their sons and daughters. They were instrumental in the creation of the activities in this book. Greg, Jesse, and Chris, we respect you and are grateful for your mission. Check out restorationproject.net.

Summit Ministries Student Conferences were life-changing for David and Jeremiah, and they can be for your teen as well. These epic two-week events challenge students ages sixteen to twenty-five to embrace God's truth and champion a Christian worldview. Students bond with other young Christians and engage with top thought leaders on everything from culture to identity to God's will to topics such as abortion, same-sex attraction, and socialism. See www.summit.org.